Making Sense *of* the Christian Faith

Making Sense *of* the Christian Faith

David J. Lose

AUGSBURG FORTRESS
Minneapolis

MAKING SENSE OF THE CHRISTIAN FAITH

This book is accompanied by a Leader Guide and DVD. These resources are also available for purchase online at www.augsburgfortress.org.

 Evangelical Lutheran Church in America
God's work. Our hands.

ISBN: 978-0-8066-9848-9

Editor: Scott Tunseth
Cover design: Joe Vaughan
Interior design: Ivy Palmer Skrade
Illustrations: Paul Soupiset, Toolbox Design

Library of Congress Cataloging-in-Publication Data

Lose, David J.
  Making sense of the Christian faith / David J. Lose.
    p. cm.
  ISBN 978-0-8066-9848-9 (alk. paper)
  1. Theology, Doctrinal--Popular works. 2. Apologetics. I. Title.
  BT77L8 2010
  230--dc22
                          2010031887

Manufactured in the U.S.A.

19   18   17   16   7   8   9   10

Contents

Dedication

For Jack and Katie, God's greatest gifts to me.

Acknowledgments

If the "Acknowledgments" section of books had theme songs, this one's would have to be the Beatles "With a Little Help From My Friends." While many authors describe writing as an extremely solitary endeavor, I have also regularly experienced it as tremendously collaborative. In particular, conversations—as you'll know from the first page of this book—are at the heart of the way I think and write, and so without numerous conversations with friends, colleagues, students, and family, I doubt I'd find much of value to say, let alone have the courage to go to back to the study and try to write it.

First and foremost, there are all the conversations that led to the beliefs, thoughts, and convictions that have shaped this book. I am grateful to teach at a seminary with colleagues and students who are eager to engage in spirited conversation about our shared faith. I have learned so much from all of them over the years.

Then there are the conversations about the book itself—its content, shape, and expression—and I have been blessed with friends who willingly gave of their time to read and discuss what I was trying to say and who always helped me do so better. Five deserve special note. Matt Skinner read the entire manuscript and offered countless suggestions that greatly improved both the content and form of this book. This is the second project he's read for me, and his curse is that his insight and intellect are so sharp that I have all but become dependent on his good judgment. Karoline Lewis and Andrew Root each read several chapters of the book and shared their wisdom about how to improve them, counsel

I gratefully accepted. Rolf Jacobson has taught me more about covenant and law than anyone, and so while the chief insights of that chapter are probably his, the shortcomings are undeniably my own. And Nadia Boltz-Weber was kind enough to read portions of the book on short notice and to reassure me that there was, indeed, something here worth pursuing.

Finally there are the conversations that led to the book's final form, and in this regard I am indebted to Scott Tunseth for his editorial acumen, not to mention patience and perseverance! Scott, along with his colleagues at Augsburg Fortress, not only see publishing as a God-given vocation but pursue it with equal measures of fidelity and excellence.

To all of these friends I can only sing, probably out of tune, "Oh, I get by with a little help from my friends." Or, in the language of the church, "Thank you and, even more, thank God for you."

Three other friends—well, more than friends—deserve mention. Karin, my life-long best friend, wife, and mother of our children, has my unending gratitude for her support, companionship, and unfailing grace while balancing so many responsibilities at work and home so well. Katie and Jack, my children, are regular reminders of God's unending goodness, mercy, and grace. I dedicate this book to them with gratitude for what they add to my life each and every day, in anticipation of the contribution they will make to God's world, and in the hope and confidence that as they grow they will not only make this Christian story their own but continue to tell and live it.

Introduction

You're probably familiar with this scenario: you're at the doctor's office, and she is reviewing with you a diagnosis and plan of treatment for whatever brought you there. You're following most of what she's saying, but from time to time there are terms that escape you. You know she's using medical lingo, but because you trust your doctor you're not too concerned. Still, it's never fun feeling like you don't fully understand what's going on, especially when it comes to your health.

Or maybe it's not the doctor's office; it's the local garage, and you have a sense of what's wrong with your car but you can't follow all of it. Again, because you trust your mechanic it's not too bad, but it would be nice to understand more, especially when it's going to cost so much.

Or maybe it's . . . Well, you get the picture. Lingo, or technical jargon, is a part of life in our modern world that we regularly accept. We know that every profession has its own vocabulary, and we know that none of us can master the language of all these different disciplines, so we trust the professionals. Typically, we're satisfied if we know enough to follow what's going on, and we're usually very grateful for the professional who can translate the jargon into every day speech—the doctor who takes the extra five minutes to make sure we really do understand the nature and impact of the surgical procedure she's recommending, or the mechanic who can create for us a picture of what's wrong with the car and what he's going to do to repair it. The opposite is also true. If we regularly don't understand our doctor or mechanic and what they are recommending or doing, we can grow frustrated and seek out someone who can help us.

Something like this also often occurs in our life in the church. There are a lot of theological terms that church professionals and theologians use that we're not familiar with. Many times that's okay. We trust them and don't need to know the difference, perhaps, between Sabellianism and Manichaeism (two ancient heresies, by the way). At other times, however, not understanding what our pastor is saying or what we're reading in the Bible can be quite frustrating. If this happens enough, we may feel out of the loop. We may wonder if what the church is talking about really affects our daily lives, or we may feel just lost enough that we wonder if trying to understand is worth our time. This can affect our interest in participating fully in our congregation or community of faith.

If you're just curious about God and the life of faith, then this book is for you.

If you have ever felt like this way and wished you knew just a little more about the Christian faith, or if you want to go more deeply into what you already know, or if you want to make sense of some of the many theological books and movies that seem to be so popular now, or if you're just curious about God and the life of faith, then this book is for you. By looking at seven central parts of the Christian story, which are sometimes called "theological doctrines," we will together explore the heart of the Christian faith and wonder together about just how important that faith can be to our everyday lives.

The Story Behind the Story

Christianity is many things. It is one of the world's great religions. It is a way of life. It is a community gathered around the belief that God acted uniquely in Jesus Christ to save the world. All of these things are true about Christianity.

But have you ever thought about Christianity as a story—a story about God, about the world, about human beings, and about the relationship between all three? The Christian faith, at a pretty basic level, is a story that tries to make sense of just about *everything*—where things came from, what meaning and purpose we have, where things are going, and so forth.

Christians have told their story in the Bible, a book that's both very important and occasionally confusing. It's important because it's the main place we turn again and again to find the heart of the Christian story. But the Bible can occasionally be frustrating, because it's not like most of the books we're familiar with. For instance, it contains many different kinds of literature—stories, parables, letters, prophecies, genealogies, legal codes, and visions of the end of the world, to name only some. The Bible was also written over many centuries and in cultures and languages that are very different from our own. And the Bible offers a number of different points of view about God, Jesus, the church, and so on. (Ever wonder, for instance, why there are four Gospel accounts of Jesus' life instead of just one?) This diversity of literary types, cultural contexts, and theological points of view can make it difficult at times to understand what holds all the different books in the Bible together.

Enter Theology

This is where theology comes in. Theology, at its best, is an attempt to make sense of the all the different confessions of faith in the Bible. (For some readers, thinking of the Bible as a collection of confessions of faith may be new. If so, you may enjoy reading *Making Sense of Scripture*.) Theology helps us sort through all the many and varied stories *in* the Bible so that we can hear the story *of* the Bible. Ultimately, what holds all the different books of the Bible together is that they are all written by people who were so gripped by their experience of God they had to tell someone about it. So if we read the Bible with care, what emerges from all these different confessions of faith is a pretty exciting story about God and the people of God.

Theology helps us sort through all the many and varied stories in the Bible.

Theology is essentially a guide to this story. Major theological doctrines are like the significant turning points or plot movements in the biblical story. Or, if you think about the Bible as a journey that begins with creation, moves through the history of Israel to the story Jesus and the early church, and ends with the story of God's creating a new heaven and earth, then theological doctrines are like the major road signs or directional markers along the path of that journey. Knowing just a little bit about the important parts of the story can help you read it—and live it—with much greater understanding and enjoyment.

Three Convictions

But before jumping into the heart of the book, I'd like to name three convictions up front.

1. I believe that all of us are, at heart, theologians. I know that may feel like a stretch. In fact, for many Christians, the word "theology" can feel intimidating. But I believe that we should take the word itself seriously. Translated most literally, *theology* simply means "words about God." So if you've ever wondered about God, if you've ever tried to make sense of Scripture, or if you've ever wondered how something you read about in the Bible impacts your life, then you've done theology.

This book is written to help you do theology better by introducing you to some of the central beliefs of the Christian faith. My hope is that by learning a little bit about what Christians through the centuries have thought about God and the work of God in the world, you'll not only recognize that you are doing theology but do it with greater confidence and enjoyment. This, in turn, may also help you get more out of church, help you understand your life in light of your faith, make it easier for you to talk with others about faith, and enrich your devotional Bible reading and prayer life.

2. Theology is never neutral. What we believe about God, humanity, and the world is very much shaped by what we have experienced of God, humanity, and the world. All of the great theologians, including the theologians who wrote the Bible, wrote out of their experience. That doesn't mean that theology is always private or uniquely personal. In fact, theology, like the Bible, is best understood when done with others. When we gather with other Christians in worship and listen to the theological convictions of other Christians through the centuries, we can learn a lot about the faith we share. But we also need to recognize that theology is always done with a point of view. And that is true of the theology I will be sharing in this book. I believe that what I am writing about is at the heart and center of the Christian faith, what C. S. Lewis once described as "mere Christianity," the kind of stuff all Christians agree to. At the same time, I recognize that not all Christians will agree with what I'm saying, and you may wonder about it, too. That's okay. As I said, part of what shapes our faith is our own experience, and I hope you will do two things as you participate in this study: a) take your experiences seriously, and b) give the points of view offered here a fair hearing.

3. I believe asking questions is essential to the life of faith. Questions are not the mark of an inadequate faith, but instead are the mark of the kind of curious, searching, seeking faith that you find all over the pages of the Bible. Faith, I think, is inherently and intensely relational, which means that faith is closer to love and trust than it is knowledge and facts. That means that the life of faith will always contain a certain element of mystery, just as our most important relationships are always a bit mysterious even while being so familiar. So if you are looking for all the answers or hope to find a set of rules that Christians should live by, this probably isn't the book for you. But if you believe, with me, that the Christian life should take seriously both our heads and our hearts, our doubts and our faith, and involves as many questions as it does answers, then I invite you to read on and explore the heart of the Christian faith.

The book is presented as a conversation in order to make it accessible and to highlight the importance of questions. Questions, as I'm sure you've noticed in your own life, are the engine of all our best conversation. Most of what we've learned about life we've learned through the give and take of asking and trying to answer questions that matter to us. And that's what we'll do here, too, asking and trying to answer questions about God and God's relationship to us and the world. Some of these questions may be very personal—why did something bad happen to someone I love? Others may not have a definitive answer—why is there so much evil and suffering in the world? But by asking and trying to answer them, we may discover that we have reservoirs of faith, hope, and courage that we didn't know existed.

As You Read

Being aware of three elements of the book may help you read it with greater enjoyment. First, *the book explores seven major theological doctrines of the faith in the order of the biblical story.* This isn't quite the same as offering a commentary on the Bible in the order of the various biblical books, starting with Genesis and moving straight through to Revelation, for instance. The Apostle Paul, as it turns out, has something to tell us about creation and sin, and we will find some things from the Old Testament prophets helpful in thinking about how God brings history and the world to a good end and a new beginning. So we are not following the Bible book by book, but rather following its larger story of the history of the world. My hope is that by the end of your reading, you'll not only have a much deeper grasp on the central elements of the Christian faith, but you'll also know the biblical story much better. If, as you're reading, you get curious about a particular part of the Bible, feel free to put this book aside and pick up the Bible to read further; you won't ever be disappointed, and you may return to this book with more questions and insights.

Second, *the book is written as a conversation* in order to invite you to "jump into" the conversation and is meant to stimulate your own thinking more than to persuade you to a particular point of view. For years, we have thought about the IQ Test as a measurement of intelligence that tests what we already know. I've often thought that a more interesting measure of intelligence might be a measure of what we are currently discovering and learning. For this reason, at the end of each chapter, there is space for you to jot down your insights and your questions. I encourage you to do so. I think you'll learn a lot and remember it better.

Third, *the book is written as a single narrative* that anyone can read with great enjoyment and satisfaction. At the same time, there are study materials available that make the book ideal for use in a group. If you'd like to read it in a group, you can find more information about the study materials at www.augsburgfortress.org.

I hope that you enjoy what I've written here. I hope that it spurs your own thoughts and conversations about God. Even more, I hope it draws you more deeply into your relationship with God and with each other. As it turns out, and as we'll discover through this narrative, that's what God is most interested in, too—that we have rich, deep, and meaningful relationships with God and each other. Blessings on your reading!

CHAPTER 1

God Talk

Theology

So, I'd like to learn more about the Christian faith.

That's great. I'd be happy to talk with you about that.

I know some things. My parents took me to church when I was a kid. But to be honest, I haven't gone much since growing up. I still think of myself as a Christian, more or less, but I'm not sure I'm a very good one.

Okay. I'm curious, though: What's prompting your interest now?

Some friends of mine had a baby a couple of months ago and invited me to the baptism. These are the first friends of ours from college to have kids, so many from my old circle of friends were there.

Was it a good time?

Definitely. But it was also kind of weird. I mean, one of my friends is very conservative, and he doesn't believe in baptizing babies.

He said that?

Not to the parents, but we drove to the service together and he told me that's what he thought. Some other friends don't go to church at all, and I have no idea what they thought about the whole deal. I got the sense they thought it was a quaint little ceremony.

And what did you think?

That was odd, too, because it all seemed really familiar—like from when I was a kid—and at the same time not familiar at all. I realized there's a lot about my own religion that I just don't know much about.

And it's important to you to know more?

Yes. I'd like to have kids someday, too, and if I have them baptized, I want to understand what it means and believe it. You know, I actually asked my friends who had the baby what the different parts of the baptism ceremony meant. They go to church fairly regularly, but they had a pretty hard time explaining it themselves.

I think it's probably not all that uncommon, even for people who go to church regularly, not to understand everything that happens there.

Well, it actually made me feel a little better to know I wasn't the only one who didn't know what was going on. I've been doing some reading since then—some about the Christian faith, but also stuff that's about spirituality in general and some books by people who don't believe in God at all.

And what do you think?

That I'd like to know a little more about the tradition I grew up in before I make any decisions.

I'm happy to help with that in whatever way I can. It seems like the baptism you attended has really sparked some soul-searching.

To tell you the truth, it's not the only thing. On the whole, it's been a pretty hard year.

We don't have to go into it if you don't want to.

No, it's all right. I think it will help if you know what's going on.

Then I'm happy to listen.

A little over a year ago, one of my best friends was in a car accident. She was hit by a drunk driver and is now paralyzed from the waist down.

That's awful. I'm really sorry to hear that.

Thanks. It really has been awful. I've been visiting her a lot, and I can't get over how much this stupid accident has cost her. She's had to work so hard, and she's had to deal with so much pain. She's not even close to living on her own yet. Even if she's able to accomplish that, her life will never be the same. It just seems so unbelievably unfair.

And you'd like some answers.

Yes. I don't know if there are answers, but I know I want to understand this all a little better.

I think that's an understandable response to this kind of accident.

And it's not just that. A few weeks ago, my mom called to say that my dad has lung cancer. He smoked when he was younger, but he quit when we were little, so maybe this shouldn't be so unexpected. Still, he's not that old and it's kind of frightening.

How is he doing?

They caught it pretty early, but cancer runs in our family, so it's hard to know how things will go. At least he's got great doctors.

How is the rest of the family dealing with it?

My dad plays it down; I think he's a little numb. My mom, though, is pretty anxious. I've got two siblings. My older sister goes to church all the time. In some ways she's like the friend I drove to the baptism; maybe a little *too* Christian for me, always explaining everything as part of God's will. When she said something like that to my younger brother about Dad's cancer, he nearly exploded. My brother is definitely not religious and he says he doesn't understand how my sister can believe in a God who lets things like this happen.

It really has been a difficult year.

Lousy, actually. And yet I know other people have it hard, too. Some people are out of work and others are in bad relationships. I know things could be a lot worse, but often I still wish they were a whole lot better.

I can totally understand that. How are you doing with all of this personally?

Some days better than others. I'm not sure what to think of it all, so mostly I've just been trying to help out—visiting my friend, helping my parents, trying to keep peace between my siblings. But I would like to understand it better.

What's been most helpful so far?

You know, it's probably been the time spent with my friend, the one who was in the accident. She's gone through stages of being really mad, and really sad, and all the rest, but she's also got this kind of quiet but amazing faith. It's not like my sister, who can explain everything away. It's more just like this confidence that things will, in the long run, be all right. I'm actually a little envious.

Say a little more.

Sometimes when I'm with my friend, she'll ask me to read something from her Bible, or she'll hum part of a familiar piece of church music, like "Amazing Grace," and I find it kind of comforting.

A lot of people find comfort in reading the Bible or in church hymns.

At other times, though . . .

Yes?

Well, I guess I don't want to believe just because things are hard. You know what I mean? I don't want to end up with some big psychological crutch, some false hope because I can't handle the truth.

The truth?

That maybe there isn't any God. That maybe this life is all we've got.

Is that what you think your friend's faith is—a psychological crutch, a false hope because life's been really hard on her?

No, absolutely not. She is very sincere, and you can tell what a difference her faith makes to her. But it doesn't seem to come that easily for me. I don't seem

to be like her. But I haven't quite given up yet, either, like I think my brother has.

There are certainly people who seem to believe very easily—though we may never know for sure how hard it is at times for someone who's gone through as much as your friend. But for others of us, faith can be a lot harder.

You said "us." Is it hard for you as well?

Sometimes when things are really hard for me or for people I care about, it's harder to believe. And at other times, all I have to do is read the newspaper and see all the pain and suffering in the world to feel like faith is very hard. But then, there are those times when faith helps me make sense of things, even hard things.

I appreciate knowing that, though I wish I had more moments when things felt like they made a little more sense.

Maybe our conversation can help with that.

Maybe. But . . .

But what? You can say it, whatever it is.

Well, like I said, I've been doing a lot of reading of late. And it just seems there are a lot of things about the Christian faith that are a little hard to swallow.

Like?

Well, like talk about a good God but seeing things like my friend's accident. Or hearing about miracle stories in the Bible but not really seeing any in real life.

Those are really big questions and, again, totally understandable given what you've gone through with your friend and your family.

I guess it just feels like a lot of things Christians seem to believe—miracles, the idea that Jesus was both a human and God, the resurrection—well, when you stop to really think about it, they all seem just a little . . .

Hard to believe? Crazy? A little out there?

Well, yes, actually. I really hope I haven't offended you by saying that.

Don't worry, you haven't. You might be interested to know, though, that the earliest Christians thought the same thing.

Are you serious?

Absolutely. It's right there in the Bible.

Where?

Actually, it's in all four of the Gospels. Each one says that when the disciples first heard that Jesus had been raised from the dead, for instance, they didn't believe.

Really?

Really. All four say more or less the same thing: those people who were closest to Jesus still had a really hard time believing that he was alive.

I don't remember learning about that in Sunday school.

Who knows, you might not have been taught it. But it's there. Listen to this story from Luke:

> But on the first day of the week, at early dawn, they came to the tomb, taking the spices that they had prepared. They found the stone rolled away from the tomb, but when they went in, they did not find the body. While they were perplexed about this, suddenly two men in dazzling clothes stood beside them. The women were terrified and bowed their faces to the ground, but the men said to them, "Why do you look for the living among the dead? He is not here, but has risen. Remember how he told you, while he was still in Galilee, that the Son of Man must be handed over to sinners, and be crucified, and on the third day rise again." Then they remembered his words, and returning from the tomb, they told all this to the eleven and to all the rest. Now it was Mary Magdalene, Joanna, Mary the mother of James, and the other women with them who told this to the apostles. But these words seemed to them an idle tale, and they did not believe them. (Luke 24:1-11)

Wow. They really didn't believe it. They thought it was an idle tale.

It's actually better than that. The word in Greek that Luke uses literally means "absolute nonsense," even "crazy talk." It's the root of our word "delirious."

I had no idea. But they must have believed at some point—right?

In time the disciples do, though not everyone around them does.

The ones who do believe, the disciples, how do they do it?

Well, that's one of the really interesting things. Again, in all four Gospels, the text mentions the early disciples being together a lot— sometimes hiding together when they were afraid, sometimes walking home together, sometimes fishing or eating together. But they're always together. And I think that's really important.

Why?

Because I think that it hints at the fact that faith is really hard to do alone. You need company. You need other people to talk with—to share your questions and doubts, and to hear their faith and hopes. Or, at other times, to listen to their doubts and share your faith. However you slice it, faith is something that takes help.

That's part of why I really appreciate your sharing all this with me. I think it's really great that you're interested in all this, and I'll be happy to help in any way I can.

Well, I'd definitely appreciate the company. I'll warn you, though, some of my questions are probably pretty simple, maybe even dumb. I really don't want to waste your time.

You won't, honestly. And I really don't think any of your questions will be dumb. Frankly, I think questions are awesome. How are you supposed to learn something if you don't ask?

Not everyone thinks that.

Maybe not, but I do. I think questions demonstrate a curious mind and are a key ingredient to a deep faith.

I'm not sure I'd describe myself as having a "deep" faith, or even much faith at all. Sometimes, as you can probably tell, I've got a whole lot more doubt than faith.

That's even better.

Are you making fun of me?

Absolutely not. That's something I won't do, I promise. I might tease you a little, or joke with you—and I'll expect and look forward to the same from you—but I won't make fun of you.

Okay, thanks.

You're welcome.

So anyway, what I really meant about doubts being good is simply that doubts are a natural, and even important, part of faith.

What do you mean? I always thought faith was the opposite of doubt.

No way. That's why the story of the disciples not believing at first is so important. Even the most "faithful" people in the Bible have doubts. Think about it: If you don't have any doubts—if you just *know* something is true—then where does the faith come in?

I've never thought of it that way.

You can learn and know certain facts—"Two plus two equals four," or "You derive the circumference of a sphere by multiplying its diameter by *pi*," or "Lincoln was the fifteenth president of the United States." But none of that takes faith. That's knowledge.

Actually . . .

What?

Well, actually, Lincoln was the *sixteenth* president of the United States. Buchanan was the fifteenth.

Oh, right. Thanks.

Well, there you go. Knowledge is something you can verify, something you can prove. It's a matter of facts. Faith, on the other hand, is believing something in the absence of all the facts, of trusting something is true even if you don't have full knowledge.

But facts are still important, right? We're not saying that we ought to believe things in spite of the facts?

Facts are definitely still important. And I wouldn't want to define faith as believing ridiculous things *because* there are no facts. But as important as they are, facts only get you so far.

What do you mean?

Well, let's go big and talk about the meaning of life.

Huh?

What's the meaning of life? You know, its ultimate purpose or goal. Or, if you want to go just a little smaller, a little more personal: what's the meaning of *your* life in particular? Do you have a purpose?

Well, that's kind of hard to answer. It's definitely something I think about from time to time. I guess everyone does. But I'm not sure I could explain it all. And now that I think of it, I definitely couldn't prove it. I mean, it's a really big question.

It definitely is, and it's one you won't answer with facts. You could tell me all kinds of things about yourself that I could verify—where you grew up, the elementary school you attended, your political affiliation, your height and weight . . .

Hold on—let's not get *too* personal!

I didn't say we *would* verify your weight, just that we could.
    But seriously, do you follow what I mean?

Yes, that actually makes a lot of sense. Facts matter, but they don't do everything.

Exactly. Facts are very helpful—when you want to balance your checkbook, fix the brakes on your car, do a math problem, or figure out who was the sixteenth president. But when it comes to the really big questions, the questions about meaning, purpose, destiny, and the rest, then facts may be interesting and even helpful. In the end, the things you say about these kinds of questions are a matter of conviction, of belief, of faith.

So you may have very good reasons for what you believe, but in the end you can't prove it. And you may see or discover things that cause you to rethink your beliefs, but in the end they're still beliefs. You still can't prove them.

Exactly. Which means that questions and doubts are both part of the life of faith.

Very interesting. But I have a question.

Shoot.

Well, this all makes faith seem like something of a head trip—it's all about what we think. But with my friend—who's very smart, by the way— it's also a lot about what she's feeling.

That's a great point. Faith is certainly about some of the things we think, which is why we're comparing it with facts, but it's also about what we *feel*. In this sense, faith is very relational, very much about trust. Like the kind of trust you put in someone when you say, "I have faith in you," or "I believe in you."

That makes sense.

In some ways, this relational sense of trust is very much at the heart of the Christian faith. That's why the creeds—the "belief statements" you sometimes say during a church service—begin with "I believe *in* God. . . ." Faith is not so much about whether you believe there *is* a God as it is about a relationship *with* God.

Could you say that again? If you aren't sure there is a God, how can you have a relationship with God?

Okay. Maybe another way to say it is this: Faith isn't about trying to prove God exists. Faith is about being in a relationship with God.

And relationships can sometimes involve doubt. Is that what you're saying?

Definitely. We've all had moments when we don't trust someone else, and that doesn't feel very good.

I think that's why doubt can be painful. I know that when I wonder if God exists, life feels a little lonelier. But when I don't trust God, or feel disappointed that God would let something bad happen to a good person, then life's not just lonely; it's sadder, more personally hard.

I totally agree.

But here we are talking about not trusting God, asking whether there even *is* a God. Are you sure that's okay?

I figure if it was okay for the disciples, it's okay for us.

That definitely makes it easier to imagine sharing some of my questions and even my doubts. But what if I don't believe what you do when we're done?

That's okay. I can't force you to believe like I do, and I wouldn't want to. Faith is a lot like hope, trust, and love. These are things you just can't force, and if you try, it actually backfires.

Here's the thing: I want to help because I like and respect you. But if, in the end, all I care about is whether you believe just like I do, then I can't really say I care about you as a person all that much, can I?

I appreciate that. A lot, actually. Not all Christians—including my sister, unfortunately—come across that way. Sometimes it seems like what matters most to them—maybe the only thing that matters—is if I believe what they say.

Well, Christians are pretty invested in what we believe. I know I am. Frankly, I think all of us—Christian or not—are invested in what we believe. It's why we believe it in the first place. At the same time, though, I think it's really important to respect you as you are and to respect where you're at.

I appreciate that, too. Thanks very much.

You're very welcome.

The bottom line for me, I guess, is that *not* believing—or, I should say, believing something else—also takes faith.

What do you mean? Is this another way of saying that knowledge and facts only get you so far?

That's right. We simply can't know everything, so there's always something we have to take on faith. For instance, even at the bottom of the most complex mathematical proofs there are axioms, unproven—actually, unprovable!—assumptions that the mathematician trusts.

So even scientists and mathematicians trying to prove some new theory have to take some things on faith?

That's right. If certain problems can't be solved, a mathematician might question those axiomatic beliefs, but there's still no getting away from having to have a little faith resting at the bottom of every system of knowledge we work with.

And the same is true when it comes to trusting people.

What do you mean?

Just that we can't know everything about a person, either. So when you're in a relationship with someone—even a very close relationship—you eventually have to trust that person or not.

Sometimes I've been disappointed by the people I trust.

We all have—which is what makes relationships risky. And it's what makes faith risky, too. There's a definite chance of being disappointed. But that's exactly why even if I disagree with some of your faith claims, I can still respect that you have faith in the first place. Because I know that having faith—believing in something you can't prove, trusting in someone you can never know fully—takes some courage.

That doesn't sound like what I've heard most people say. And not only from Christians. I've seen some of the recent books by atheists like Richard Dawkins and Christopher Hitchens. They seem to think faith is just plain bad, and the less you have of it the better.

I think they are referring to religious faith in particular. But to be honest, I don't think they describe the faith and actions of most Christians very fairly. I can't say I'm all that attracted to the absolutist, fundamentalist faith they talk about either, but most of the Christians I know aren't like that.

No, that's true. My friend from college—the one who doesn't believe in baptizing babies—and my sister sometimes seem a little extreme, but even they don't seem quite as off the wall as the Christians those guys are talking about.

Also, I don't know if those authors recognize that at the bottom of their own systems of knowledge—whether of biology, evolution, or philosophy—there are things they take on faith, too. Maybe they really do think they can prove God doesn't exist, just as some fundamentalist Christians think they can prove God does. But, frankly, I don't find either extreme particularly helpful or, for that matter, attractive.

Neither do I.

Now, what's kind of interesting is that I actually believe that faith includes doubts and that I should respect you even if we disagree about important matters of faith because of the faith tradition I come out of. But not all the different traditions of Christianity see things this way, which might be why you haven't experienced this from some Christians.

So Christians don't agree on all this stuff.

Definitely not. I mean, there's a ton of stuff that Christians do agree on—particularly about Jesus Christ. That's why it's called Christianity. But there are also lots of things that Christians disagree on—ironically, also often about Jesus! This is what makes theology so important: it describes the way Christians try to make sense of what God is up to.

Wait a minute. Theology? I'm not sure I'm ready to do theology. That sounds a little intense.

What would you say if I told you that you are already doing theology?

I'd say you aren't thinking too straight. I'm no theologian.

Actually, at this point I'd beg to differ. Theology is, most simply, talk about God.

Come on. I thought theology was all about doctrines, the stuff you have to believe.

Theology does often deal with doctrines, but doctrine is essentially reflection on the actual experiences of Christians through the centuries. It's a way of making sense of how people experienced God in their lives and the world. If we reduce it all to memorizing certain dates or facts or forcing people to believe some kind of doctrinal laundry list, then I think we've actually missed the point of what theology is all about.

Which is . . . ?

Helping us gain a perspective on our experience of God by comparing it with the experience and reflections of other Christians through the centuries.

I really thought it would be a little more complicated than that.

Well, some of those reflections can get pretty complicated. But it doesn't always have to be. The meaning of the word *theology* might actually help us out at this point. *Theo* is Greek for "God," and *logia* comes from the Greek *logos*, meaning "words." It refers to a collection of sayings about something or, really, the study of something. So biology is, literally, the study of *bios*, "life." In the same way, theology is, most formally, the study of God, but you could also just call it God-talk, words about God. So pretty much anytime you're wondering or talking about God, you're doing theology. And when you put it that way, we're all theologians.

Theo + logos = Theology
God + words = God-talk

So anything I say about God is theology?

Sure. It doesn't mean it's good theology, but it's theology!

But seriously, on one level, all of our God-talk—whether questions, doubts, confessions of faith, or whatever— is theology. At the same time, there is a more formal or rigorous reflection on God, the

Bible, the church and its mission, and so forth. That is also theology and probably more what you were thinking of.

So how can you tell whether the theology you're doing is good or bad?

Great question. John Wesley, a British theologian who lived during the eighteenth century, thought there were four sources for theology. The Bible is the most important, because in the Bible you find the story of God and the people of God that is at the heart of Christianity. In one sense, it's the collection of the original God-talk that's foundational to all Christians. Second, there's the collection of the church's God-talk about the God-talk in the Bible.

Whoa, hold on. I get that the Bible is really important. I can't say I always understand the Bible, but I get that it's important. But I think you lost me on the God-talk about the God-talk.

Sorry. I may have been getting a little too clever. Essentially, the Bible is the collection of confessions of faith of the people of ancient Israel and the early Christians. It's the foundational or original God-talk. For the last two thousand years, though, Christians have been reflecting on what's in the Bible—thinking about it, discussing it, and sometimes arguing about it. And that theology is often called the Christian tradition, or what I called "the church's God-talk."

So the church's God-talk is always about the Bible's God-talk. I think I've got it. Bible and tradition. You said there were two others.

Yes, the third we've already mentioned, and that's our experience. We make sense of things in the Bible and in the church in relation to our own experience. So when you hear a story about someone being healed, you wonder why that doesn't happen to your friend. Or when I read something about how God is all-powerful, I may wonder why God doesn't prevent earthquakes, hurricanes, and tsunamis.

Yeah, that happens all the time, whether I want it to or not.

And it happens the other way around, too. That is, I may hear a sermon about how God works through others and think about when a friend really helped me through a hard time. Either way, whether they're causing us to doubt or have faith, our actual experiences in the world shape our theology.

That make sense. And the fourth thing?

The fourth is our reason, our intellect, our ability to think about our experience, tradition, and Scripture.

But I kind of got the idea that faith and reason were opposites, or at least opposed to each other.

Did you hear that from the celebrity atheists you mentioned, or from fundamentalist Christians?

Both, now that I think about it.

Well, I disagree. I think God gave us our brains to use. Don't get me wrong; I don't think we can simply think our way into faith. Faith, as we already said, is more like trust than knowledge. Even so, I think we should always test what we believe, and if it doesn't make sense, then there's something wrong.

Scripture, tradition, experience, and reason. This came from Wesley, the guy you mentioned.

I think a number of theologians have probably worked this way, but it's been attributed to him and, in his honor, it's even called the "Wesleyan Quadrilateral," though I wouldn't stress out too much if you can't remember the name.

Thanks, I won't.
And you said the Bible is the most important?

Yes, because it's the foundational confessions, or God-talk.

Foundational, you mean, like our country's Constitution? There are lots of new laws and customs in our country, but they all go back to that core.

In some ways, yes, the Bible is like a constitution in that it's the foundational document that we keep going back to. But to be honest, I'd actually say the Bible's a little closer to your grandmother's scrapbook than a constitution.

How did you know my grandmother had a scrapbook?

Don't all grandmothers?

Maybe. But seriously, how in the world is the Bible like a scrapbook?

First off, while we tend to think of the Bible as a single book, it's actually a collection of sixty-six books written over more than a thousand years in a number of different languages and cultures. Which means that we can't expect everything to line up quite so easily into a set of rules to live by, like we do a constitution.

That makes sense. But still, a scrapbook?

Think about it. A scrapbook is passed down through the generations and people keep adding things to it to tell the story of the family. Over time, there are all manner of things, from the letters of an immigrant to his family in the homeland, to the tickets from the movie your parents saw on their first date, to the program from your second grade play. And from all these bits and pieces emerges the story of your family, a story that continues to shape your own sense of who you are and maybe even of where you're heading.

Okay, I can see that. And this is what the Bible is?

Well, the Bible is similar to a scrapbook in a couple of ways. For instance, there are all different kinds of writing in the Bible, too, ranging from narratives like the Gospels that we're familiar with, to legal codes and genealogies, letters and love poetry—literary forms we're not always so familiar with. What emerges from all these differ-ent things is the story of God and the people of God.

Like a scrapbook, but of our spiritual family rather than our biological one.

Exactly. And what holds all the different pieces of the scrapbook together is that all of them are confessions of faith in the same God, the God of Israel and of the Christian church.

Confessions?

Right. That is, all the people who wrote the various parts of the Bible were so gripped by their experience of God that they had to share it, by telling it or writing it down. These weren't things they could prove—which might be why the one thing you won't find in the Bible is simply a list of facts or a laundry list of things you have to believe. So the things they wrote were confessions of faith.

Things they had good reason to believe but couldn't prove.

Exactly. And out of all these different confessions emerges the story of God as told by the people of God. And at the heart of that story is the hope that when we hear all these different confessions and con-versations, we'll want to join in.

To make our own confession and join the conversation about God.

Right.

Okay, that makes sense.
And just to check: what we're doing now, just talking about God, that's really theology, too.

Yup. Just check out the Bible—it's full of the ordinary God-talk we were talking about earlier.

The questions, doubts, and all?

Absolutely. From the people writing the Psalms who regularly ask God questions like, "How long, O Lord, do we have to wait for help?" or "Why do evil people prosper and good people suffer?" to the prophets getting downright angry at times with God, to Jesus' own cry of doubt and despair. The Bible is full of very human emotions—questions and doubts, as well as confessions of faith and prayers of thanksgiving. It's all there.

Jesus had doubts?

On the cross he cries out, "My God, my God, why have you forsaken me?" And if Jesus can say these kinds of things, I don't see why we can't be just as honest in our God-talk.

That's very helpful. Maybe I can do theology after all, and maybe that's what I really do want to talk about. I mean, I think my questions aren't that different from the ones you said were in the Bible: Who is God, and what is it that God expects from me? Is there a meaning or purpose to this life? Why is there suffering? And why do I sometimes feel abandoned, and what do I do about it? When I think about it, though, it seems like a huge undertaking.

It is a big undertaking, but I think you'll find it's worth the time. You'll also find you're not the only person with questions, and so you don't have to do it all alone. You may find that talking about these questions with another person—whether it's me or someone else you trust—or discussing them with a group of people can even be fun.

Well, this *is* kind of fun. But if you'd told me yesterday that I'd be doing theology today—and enjoying it—I wouldn't have believed you.

I know what you mean. You never quite know where the next day is going to take you, or what God might do with it.

God? You think God is a part of all this? I thought we were only talking *about* God.

We are talking about God. But I think that God is at work in and through our conversation. Admittedly, that's a part of my faith, and not something I can prove, but I believe that God works through and even meets us in our questions and conversation.

Hmm . . . I wonder if I should find the idea of meeting God a little alarming. At least, isn't that the reaction when people talk about "meeting your maker"?!

Well, I did say that faith—and that includes thinking about faith—can be risky business.

True enough.

But to be honest, I find the idea that God likes questions kind of encouraging. Maybe I would be interested in meeting a God who doesn't disapprove of questions but actually uses them to connect with us. It's not something you hear about that often.

Maybe not, but in talking about it, we're right at the heart of what theology is all about.

What do you mean?

Just that when we're trying to figure out what God is like, we really are doing significant God-talk. I mean, is God curious or does God know everything? Is God all-powerful or vulnerable? Is God joyful or vengeful, patient or impatient, loving or stern? These are some of the really central questions of theology.

That's interesting. I think if you asked most people what the main point of doing theology is, they'd probably say it's to prove to you that God exists.

Some Christian theologians are very interested in that question. But to be honest, I'm not sure you really can prove whether God exists. Some pretty famous theologians have tried, but I suspect the arguments work best for the people who already believe.

I hadn't thought of that. But I guess it's like trying to convince someone to fall in love with you. I mean, if the person loves you, all the reasons seem pretty obvious and persuasive. But if the person isn't in love with you, not only are the reasons you give not convincing, but arguing about it might make you look a little silly.

That's a good analogy, because faith really is like a relationship. So, for me, theology is less about trying to prove a point and more about what we've been doing already—describing how we think about God in relation to what we read in the Bible, hear in church, experience in the world, and think with our brains.

Back to the Quadrilateral.

I'm impressed you remembered.

And, yes, this kind of theological thinking, or God-talk, is really important. After all, how we think of God—as just, loving, angry, stern, threatening, tender, or some combination of these—is definitely going to shape our view of the world, of ourselves, and of each other. And more likely than not, it will really affect the way we relate to others.

So what if we come to different answers about these questions. Is that really okay?

Definitely. Sometimes our answers will be different. But at many other times they will be similar. And sometimes my answer might help you shape yours.

And mine might affect yours?

Definitely. That's why from the time of the disciples on, theology—God-talk—is better done with company.

When you put it that way, I think I'm ready to do it.

Great, but before we jump into everything, there are two other things about theology I'd like to touch on briefly. I think they may help our conversation.

Okay.

First, all theology is done from a personal perspective, a point of view. Who I am and what I've experienced shape how I think about theology.

That makes sense. After all, part of the reason I'm interested in theology at all right now is what's been happening with my dad and my friends, both the one who had the accident and the ones who just had their baby. All of this shapes my questions.

Right. Which is one of the reasons different Christians think about their faith differently. We've had different experiences and learned different things. We may read the same Bible, but all of the things that make us who we are shape the lens we each use when we read the same book. So it's important to realize that the things I say may reflect a broad strand of Christianity, but there will be others who might answer very differently.

That's fair. I appreciate you recognizing that your view maybe isn't the one true way to think about God.

Oh, don't get me wrong, I definitely think my theology is the right one, but I also realize that everyone else does, too! I mean, if I didn't believe it was right, I wouldn't believe it. At the same time, I realize that faithful Christians can disagree and, even more, that there are usually some valuable things in the positions I disagree with. Does that make sense?

Yeah. We believe what we believe for a reason, but that doesn't mean we can't acknowledge that other people have good reasons for what they believe or that we can learn from them.

Exactly. Okay, second, there are limits to theology.

What do you mean?

Just that theology can't answer everything. The question of suffering and your friend's accident that got you started thinking about a lot of this stuff, for instance. I'm not sure that's a question we, or anyone for that matter, can fully or completely answer.

That can be a little frustrating.

No question, although not having a definite answer doesn't mean we don't have anything to say.

What do you mean?

We can give a perspective on evil and suffering. We can provide a helpful framework to think though these questions. We can put our questions alongside the questions and answers many faithful people have given down through the ages. And we can offer hope during times of suffering and motivation to resist the evil we see around us that causes suffering. But I don't know if we can ever give a definitive answer.

That actually sounds kind of like what my friend says. Once I asked her why she thought all this happened, and she said she wasn't sure there was a good answer, but that she was sure glad I was there with her in the middle of the questions.

I think that's right. Theology, at its best, is a communal practice. And some things are just too big to settle with simple answers. Life is more complicated than a television sitcom, where everything has to be resolved in thirty minutes.

So what do you do when you get to one of those questions you can't answer?

You read the biblical story as closely as you can, you talk about it with other Christians, and you pray. All of these things might give you some insight that you wouldn't have otherwise, and all of them also help you live with some of the questions that don't seem to have answers.

I guess there are some questions that we may not get answered until we can put them to God face-to-face.

Phrased that way, maybe there are some questions we can wait to have answered!

Definitely. But in the meantime . . .

Yes, in the meantime, there's a lot we can talk about. Where do you want to begin?

You know, I've got so many questions I'm not even sure where to start!

Then can I make a suggestion?

Sure.

How about if we start at the beginning?

What do you mean?

Well, I've been thinking that maybe the best way to get at this—the bigger question of what Christians really believe—is to trace the story of God and the people of God that the Bible tells. To dive into the family scrapbook, as it were, and see where it leads us. We can't cover it all, for sure, but maybe we can hit the major points of the plotline, so to speak, of the biblical drama, and cover a number of questions you might have—and probably some you haven't even thought about yet.

That sounds like a very good idea. I have a Bible, and I've even read it a little, though I can't say I always understand it.

No problem. Maybe going through its story will help it make a little more sense.

Sounds good.

Then I think the place to begin really is the beginning, as in, "In the beginning, God created the heavens and the earth."

I'm looking forward to it.

Insights and Questions

CHAPTER **2**

Original Blessing

Creation

So, you said you wanted to begin at the beginning with creation.

I think that's probably a helpful place to get started.

That makes sense, although I have to admit it also makes me a little nervous.

How come?

Because it seems these days that so many people get worked up about creation. I've watched news reports about the school board fights and protests about teaching creation along with evolution in school, and I've heard these same arguments around our supper table when my sister and brother start going at it. So I have to say that if that's why we're starting with creation, I'm not that interested in going there.

No problem. That's definitely *not* why I want to start at the beginning.

Really? But what else is there to talk about? Those are the big questions, right? How God created everything and whether it was through evolution or in six days.

Those are important questions, but there are other important things to talk about as well. Like, for instance, who is God really? What are the role and purpose of humanity? And what's the relationship between God as creator and us as creation?

Okay, okay, I get the picture! There's more than the creation-evolution discussion.

Exactly.

I'm actually glad to start somewhere else.

All right, let's see if you can place this line: "In the beginning God made the heavens and the earth."

That's the way the Bible starts off, isn't it?

Right. It's one of the great opening lines in literature.

Right up there with "It was the best of times, it was the worst of times."

It's interesting you mention Dickens's *A Tale of Two Cities*. Because I think how you begin something is really important. It tells you a lot about what's going to come. So Dickens totally sets the tone of his book with that long and carefully crafted first line. I mean, you don't know at all what's coming, but you know it's going to be a bumpy ride.

I think something similar is going on with the Bible.

What do you mean?

I think that opening line tells us something important about both the Bible and God.

Okay, I'll bite: What does it tell us about the Bible?

That this is one seriously big story.

Because . . . ?

Because it begins at the very, very beginning. I mean, there's kind of an audacity about saying your story starts at the very beginning—like the story you're about to start is *the* story, the ultimate story, the story that comes before all other stories and holds all of them within it.

And it follows up on the claim by ending . . .

Let me guess, at the end?

The *very* end. That's right. The Bible starts at the very beginning and ends at the very end.

Okay, so it's a really big story. I'm still not totally sure why that's such a big deal.

Because, written this way, the Bible invites us to see ourselves as part of the story, connected to all the characters we're about to read about. The story begins at the beginning, with the creation of the world, and then, as we'll see, it tells the story of the people of Israel in the Old Testament, of Jesus in the four Gospels, and of the early church in a book called the Acts of the Apostles and a number of early letters, and then it stops. Except it doesn't stop, because then it jumps to the very end of history in a book called Revelation. Which means the Bible tells this really big story that begins at the very beginning and ends at the very end, and we all live out our lives somewhere between the Acts of the Apostles and Revelation.

Which means that, according to the Bible, we're all characters in this ongoing story?

That's right.

Interesting. If that's true, then I have to say I agree with you—this *is* one big story. I'm not sure I quite get where you're going with this yet.

That's okay. It's enough that you're willing to go along for the ride.

That I can do.

So, if that's what the first line tells us about the Bible, what does it tell us about God?

That God creates.

I kind of gathered that.

Yeah, but think about it. The very first thing we learn about God is that God is creative, that God wants to make things, that God sets things in motion. Not that God is passive, or distant, or destructive, or indifferent, or anything else, but that God *creates*. And that only continues in the rest of this first story of creation.

First story of creation? You mean there's more than one?

There are two, actually. The first begins, well, in the beginning and tells the story of creation in terms of six days during which God crafted the heavens and the earth, light and darkness, seas and dry land, all the animals, and finally human beings. And all of it, God says, is good, even very good.

I think that's the one I'm familiar with.

Have you ever heard of Adam and Eve?

Of course.

Well, they're not in that one.

You're kidding.

Nope. This first story of creation, which probably is pretty familiar and runs from Genesis 1:1 through 2:4, ends with God resting on the seventh day after six days of creative work, and hallowing, or making very special, the seventh day as a day of rest for all living things.

But you said God created humans during the six days.

True, but they are not named. That comes in the second story.

How can you tell it's a second story?

A couple of things. In terms of style, after the first one comes to a close with God resting on the seventh day, the second story starts with an introductory phrase—"These are the generations . . ."—that's repeated several times in the first part of Genesis, always just before the start of a new part of the story Genesis is telling. Not only that, the first creation story always uses one Hebrew word for God—*Elohim*—while the second account uses a different Hebrew word—*Yahweh Elohim*—which we translate, "the Lord God."

Interesting.

And in terms of plot: in the first story God created all the vegetation on the third day and all animals and humankind on the sixth day, while in the second story it says God created a single human, Adam, before God created any vegetation. Then God created the Garden of Eden for Adam to work. Later, searching for a suitable partner for

Adam, God creates animals and brings them to Adam to be named, but no partner is found, and so God creates Eve.

Whoa. We've got to slow down. I've got about a dozen and a half questions I want to ask.

Why don't we take them one at a time.

Okay, first up: Why two stories?

The odds are there were two stories the Israelites knew about creation. One emphasized the orderliness of creation, with its focus on the progression of God's work day after day to create and order the heavens and the earth. This story culminates with the creation of humanity on the sixth day and God resting on, and hallowing, the seventh day. This was probably a story passed down through the generations by the priests of Israel who were, after all, the caretakers of the Sabbath, Israel's sacred day of rest.

That sounds reasonable. And the second story?

It represented another tradition that wasn't so concerned with the orderliness of creation, and there's no mention of days or Sabbath. Instead, the story is very concerned with the relationship between God and humankind, represented by Adam and Eve, as well as the relationships between the humans themselves and between humanity and the rest of creation, represented by the garden and the animals. This story of creation continues by delving into what goes wrong with those relationships when it tells the story of what's often called "the fall," when Adam and Eve are tempted to disobey God.

And it didn't bother people back then that there were two different stories about the same event? That wasn't a problem?

No, it didn't bother them. In the ancient world, stories were told far more to teach and to inspire than they were offered as accurate historical or scientific records. The idea that history must be factually accurate that we're so accustomed to is a product of the seventeenth-century European Enlightenment.

So the people in the ancient world didn't read this the way we read history? Did they think there really was an Adam and Eve, or didn't they?

That's a great question. They may have, though to be honest, we don't know for sure. But that definitely wasn't the point of telling the stories. They weren't told as history as we know history, and they definitely aren't offered as scientific explanations.

Then what are they?

At heart, they're confessions of faith. Their goal is to make sense of some of the big questions in life, not to capture a reliable historical picture. And so putting two stories side by side—each offering insight into different but complementary truths about the origins of the world—would have made perfect sense.

But isn't that exactly what's causing all the commotion I mentioned earlier about teaching creation "science" in schools? Don't a lot of people today argue that we should read the Bible as scientifically accurate? And doesn't that get a lot harder if you have two different stories in creation? I mean, in one of those stories humans come last and are, it sounds like, the crowning achievement of God's work. In the other story they, or at least one of them, comes near the beginning and everything else follows.

Some Christians do take Genesis as literal history, so they would disagree that there are two distinct stories. Not only that, but they think of the Bible along the lines of a modern science textbook or history book. They assume that if there are any scientific or historical errors, then the Bible must not be trustworthy. That's why they get so concerned about creation. They feel they need to prove that the Bible is factually accurate in order to believe that it's true.

You don't seem to think of the Bible that way.

I think there are many truths that can't be proven in a laboratory, and often these are the most important ones. The importance of love and freedom, whether humans have intrinsic worth, whether our lives have any meaning—these are things we stake our lives on, but when push comes to shove, we realize we can't prove them and so we take them on faith.

This is like our discussion of facts and faith earlier. Facts are great, but they only get us so far.

Exactly. And these stories about creation are like that. They are confessions of faith, not statements of fact. When I was a kid, my parents explained it to me by saying that Genesis was far more interested in "who" than "how." And I still believe that.

What do you mean?

I just don't think the writers of the Bible were trying to give a scientific account of how the world was created. Instead, I think they were confessing their faith that God was and is the Creator. And if this is true—and I think it is—that means that reading the Bible as science is actually to read it *against* the intentions and purposes of the original authors. They were interested in sharing with us their faith in God, not in persuading us that the world was created in six chronological days, or six different ages, or in the moment of the Big Bang, or whatever. Does that make sense?

That makes a lot of sense, actually, and it helps me understand what's going on in Genesis. It's not about the mechanics of *how,* but it's about God. *Who* God is as a creator.

Exactly right.

So can I ask about something that kind of bugs me?

Sure.

Okay, so what's going on with this business of God creating Adam first and then Eve? I mean, it seems that for much of history people seemed to think that men were somehow superior to, or at least more important than, women.

37

Is this where all that stuff starts?

The story of the creation of Adam and Eve may indeed be linked to ancient views about the relationship between men and women, though I'm not sure that relationship is totally straightforward.

What do you mean?

Just that it's hard to tell whether the stories were trying to influence the way people thought or whether the stories were told to explain the way things seemed to be. In these ancient cultures, men were given more authority than women, and these stories tried to explain why.

Interesting, though I still don't think I like it.

For what it's worth, though, I tend to think that reading Genesis in either of those ways—that it supports or explains the superiority of men to women—is something of a misreading of the story.

Really? I'd be interested in hearing you say more about that.

On the one hand, there's not much doubt that the ancient Israelites shared the common assumption that men should have more authority than women, perhaps even that men should have authority over women. That point of view may be reflected in this second account of creation and, even more, in the story of the fall that comes next.

What do you make of that?

I think that this is part of what it means to say that the Bible is a collection of the confessions of faith of real human beings. Their confessions of faith were shaped by their own views of the world, of relationships, and all the rest.

But that's not the whole story?

No, it's not. Because, on the other hand, there are some interesting elements of both creation stories that we often overlook. These suggest a far more interesting picture of how the biblical authors imagined the relationship between men and women.

Like?

Well, for starters, in the first story, men and women are created together; both are created, as the Bible says, in the image of God. There is nothing unequal about it.

What about the second story?

In the second story, I think that it's really interesting that the word we translate "Adam" doesn't really imply a gender at first.

What do you mean?

The Hebrew word *adamah* means "earth." So Adam actually means "the one who comes from the earth" or, even more literally, "the earthling."

Get out!

It's true. The name refers to the second account's description of how God formed the first human from the earth, breathing life into the human. It's sort of like the relationship between our English words *humus*—which means "earthy soil"—and *human*. Humans are those who came from the humus. That's why the first creation story says that "God created *adam*—humankind—in the image of God, male and female God created them" (see Genesis 1:27). The use of *adam* in this case is neutral, referring actually to both genders.

So why do we think of Adam as male?

It's not unlike how until recently we used "man" to refer both to a specific male as well as to all humankind, both male and female. While *adam* is essentially gender-neutral at first, after the woman is created, the word *adam* is continually associated with the man, so we think of him as Adam. But that's actually a bit sloppy, because in these first couple of chapters, *adam* always has a definite article before it, and so is better translated "*the* man." Only in chapters 4 and 5 of Genesis does *adam* come without an article and so refers to a name, Adam. At the end of the story of the fall, just before the man and woman are about to leave Eden, the Bible says, "And the man—*adam*—named his wife Eve, because she was the mother of all who lived." *Eve* literally means "living."

This is all really interesting. It sheds a whole new light on the story. But what about the man coming first and the woman second? You said you thought it was a mistake to read it as meaning that the Bible supports men being somehow superior to women.

Well, again, there's no denying that this passage comes from a culture that gives men more authority than women.

At the same time, though, I don't think you can argue for the superiority of men over women from this passage in the Bible. Look, for instance, at how the emphasis in the story isn't on the distinct status of the two but rather on their partnership, on the fact that the two together fulfill something that only one could not. I think the point of this story is much more that humans are created for relationship than that the man is created first. So God says, "It is not good that the man should be alone; I will make him a helper"—in the sense of a coworker or companion—"as his partner" (Genesis 2:18).

It seems like the terms "coworker" and "partner" are important.

Yes, and so is what happens next. Because God next creates all the animals and brings them to the man to see what he will name them, and while he names them all, none of them are suitable co-workers, none of them are fit to be his partner.

I can just imagine it: Okay, Lord, I'll call this one "aardvark," but I really don't think it's going to make it as my partner.

> That's great. Which would help to explain the man's cry, "At last . . . !" when he first sees the woman. But there's one other thing to pay attention to. After finding no suitable partner among the animals, God makes the man go to sleep and forms the woman from his side, probably indicating that they are to be side by side with each other, partners. Then the man wakes up and exclaims, "This at last is bone of my bone, flesh of my flesh."

So again there's a sense that they are the same, equal, not one higher than the other.

> Right, and only at this point is a clear distinction made between male and female in the words for "woman" and "man," as if the two define each other. So at the beginning of creation, at least, humans seem to be made for relationship, understanding themselves in relation to each other, equal partners in the work God will give them.

Very interesting. Well, that definitely helps me hear that story differently. Actually, a lot better. But I'm curious what else you think this says about God. I mean, you said that the opening line tells us that God is creative. Now that we're so much further into the story, what does it tell us about God?

> Well, what do *you* hear?

Me?

> Yeah. You can also notice things, and that's essentially what really good Bible study is—slowing down enough to pay close attention to what happens: what are the significant details of the story, what are the gaps, and what does all that suggest?
>
> So what do you notice?

Well, it seems that God really does like creating. In both stories that's what's going on more than anything else. And that the humans really matter. They get the top spot in the order of creation in the first story, and the second story totally revolves around them. And it seems like God really cares about Adam. I mean, God doesn't want him to be alone and so creates and brings all the animals. And then God creates once more so that the woman can be his partner.

Those are great insights. I'd like to build on them a little.

For instance, I think you're absolutely right. God loves creating. And, I think, we can also say that God creates out of love.

What do you mean?

Well, there are a number of places in the Bible that talk about God's great love.

Like John 3:16? "For God so loved the world . . ."?

Right—the world's most famous Bible verse.

That's probably the one Bible verse I actually know by heart.

A lot of people do, and for good reason. It captures the heart of God. The Old Testament also talks about God's love, and at one point the New Testament actually says that "God is love" (1 John 4:8).

I think all this talk about love helps us understand God's work in creation. God doesn't just create in general, or because God is bored. God creates out of love, because God wants to share God's love with creation. And that includes humanity—Adam, Eve, and all of us.

That seems really important.

It is. We'll see again and again that, like you said, God really cares about humans—about all of us. The God of the Bible is all about relationships, two in particular: the relationship God has with us and the relationship we have with each other, which is why our conversation about the partnership between Adam and Eve is important. They are created to be in relationship with each other. And through their relationship with God and with each other, they are complete.

I like that. It's like Adam's not quite complete until Eve comes along. Like it really isn't good that he's alone, or for that matter that any of us are alone. It's like we're all made for relationship.

I think you're right.

There's something else that you noticed that I think is important, too.

Really—what?

You noticed that creation takes some time. And that's true in both creation accounts. In the first story it's spread across the six days, and in the second it's also done in stages, actually in response to how creation is working out so far.

How so?

Just what you said before: that God creates the man, decides it's not good for him to be alone, so creates all the animals and brings them to the man to see what he'll call them and whether a good partner can be found. And then God creates again to make woman. I mean, God creates, evaluates how creation is going, and then creates some more.

But don't you think God knows that no animal is going to be found as a suitable partner? I mean, doesn't God know everything?

That's certainly the testimony of many Christians, and many parts of the Bible support that, too. And quite frankly, I typically think that way as well. But right now I'm interested in what the story shows us. And this particular story seems less interested in whether God knows everything and a lot more interested in how God responds to the needs of the creation by *continuing* to create. Remember, Genesis isn't science; it's story, and I'm curious about what the story is trying to tell us.

Maybe that creation wasn't over in six days, or in one Big Bang instant, or whatever. Maybe God continued to be involved, continued to respond to the needs of the creation.

I think you could actually make that present tense.

How's that?

Well, you said that God *continued* to be involved—past tense—and I wonder if the story isn't saying that God continues—present tense—to be at work, continues to respond to the needs of creation, continues to respond to our need.

You mean that creation isn't done yet?

I definitely *don't* think that God just made the world, set it running, and then backed off, like a clock maker would a clock. I think God's more involved than that. So whether you want to say, "God created and still sustains the world," or "God created and is still creating the world," I think the key is noticing that, according to the Bible, God is still involved, keeps creating, caring, responding to the creation. In this sense, God's creative activity is ongoing.

I have to say that I've never thought about that before.

And this won't end in Genesis. Throughout the Bible God will make promises, give laws, warn, rescue, save—all kinds of things, some of them somewhat surprising. Later books in the Bible will not only praise God's ongoing activity, in fact, but also talk about God "doing a new thing" (Isaiah 43:19).

That's interesting. I have to say that I tend to think of creation as something that's once and done. But this is a much more dynamic sense of what it means to create.

Right. Creation both happened and still happens.

While we were talking about this, I also realized that God doesn't do it entirely alone, either. I mean the original act of creation, sure, but once humans are involved, God gives them something to do almost immediately, like inviting Adam to name all the animals.

That's right. Adam is drawn into the creative work of God right from the beginning.

And in a really important way. I mean, think about naming our kids and our pets. It's one of the most personal things we do. And Adam gets to name everything. It just seems like a huge mark of trust, even of privilege, that God involves Adam in that way.

I think so, too. And it's clear that the man and woman are to care for each other as well. That's the force of God creating a "partner." They're in this together. And it's true of not only the second creation story but the first as well, where it says:

God blessed them, and God said to them, "Be fruitful and multiply, and
fill the earth and subdue it; and have dominion over the fish of the sea
and over the birds of the air and over every living thing that moves upon
the earth." (Genesis 1:28)

**In a sense, this time it's *taming* instead of *naming*. Well, we sure seem to have
followed that command—both about multiplying as well as about subduing.**
**But that raises a question for me: What does this passage mean for the
environment? Hasn't all of our multiplying and subduing and having dominion kind of stretched things, even pushed things to the limit in terms of what
the world can support?**

That's a great question. On the one hand, there's no question that the
humans are invited into the ongoing work of creation. They're given
something important to do. They are invited right off the bat to be
God's partners, even co-creators. On the other hand, what does that
invitation look like? I suspect the answer turns on what you think
verbs like "subdue" and "have dominion" mean. Do they mean, for
instance, "doing whatever you want"? I don't think so.

What do you think they mean, then?

Both words are interesting on their own, but way more so when put
side by side like they are here. The Hebrew word translated "subdue"
has a lively sense of struggle to it. In other places in the Bible, for
instance, the word is used to describe what one army tries to do to
another. So the creation, according to this account, is wild at heart,
and humankind will need to work hard, even struggle, to bring order
to it, to make it suitable for life.

And "dominion"?

That's where things get really interesting. *Dominion* is a royal word,
something kings exercise. Throughout the Old Testament, though,
the king's job isn't only to protect the borders against enemies and
other stuff we usually associate with kings; it's also to care for the
vulnerable and promote peace. For instance, in Psalm 72, which is
offered as a prayer for King Solomon, the psalm writer first prays that
the king would "have dominion from sea to sea" and that "his foes
bow down before him," but then also continues:

For he delivers the needy when they call,
the poor and those who have no helper.
He has pity on the weak and the needy,
and saves the lives of the needy.
From oppression and violence he redeems their life;
and precious is their blood in his sight. (Psalm 72:12-14)

So the king's "dominion" is about taking care of everyone?

Right. And not only do we have these positive affirmations of the king's job in the Psalms, we also have the writings of the prophets, who regularly rail against the king when they *don't* do this kind of thing. At one point the prophet Ezekiel, for instance, describes the king as a shepherd and then accuses the kings of not being good shepherds because they've been feeding themselves instead of taking care of the poor, the weak, and the sick (Ezekiel 34:2b-4). The king, in this sense, is both shepherd and steward, the one set up by God to take care of God's people.

That puts a whole new twist on things. I mean, taming a wild creation is one thing, but if a king having dominion over people is about taking care of them, especially those who are needy, then humankind having dominion over the earth might be the same: taking care of it and protecting it, especially the parts that are most vulnerable.

Exactly.

Which brings us back to relationships again. God cares about the relationships we have not only with each other but also with the whole creation.

Right. God cares enough to invite us to "have dominion" over creation.

That's a huge job. And now that I think of it, I totally get what it means to say that the work of creation—or at least our job of taking care of creation—continues. I mean, what with taking care of each other and taking care of the earth and all its creatures, we've got a lot of work to do and probably should get started right away.

Actually, I think you already have.

What do you mean?

Well, you talked earlier about spending a lot of time with your friend since her accident. Think what an encouragement that has been. Or supporting your parents during your dad's illness. That's helping God continue the work of creation.

I see what you mean, but I guess I always thought that it would be bigger, more dramatic, like saving a rainforest or negotiating a peace treaty.

Sometimes the work we do as God's partners and co-creators may be dramatic. But it doesn't have to be. Keeping peace in a family might not be as dramatic as signing a peace treaty, but it still advances God's good will and intention for creation. And raising children who care about the earth, or striving to make your place of work more earth-friendly, might not feel as momentous as saving a rainforest, but you're still partnering in God's work. I think there are countless ways, both small and large, that we can join in God's work to care for this world.

When you put it that way, it seems like God has placed a lot of faith in us, although that seems like a funny way to put it.

What do you mean?

Well, we're supposed to have faith in God, right? But here, at the beginning of the story, it seems like God puts tremendous faith in us.

I think you're right. God's act of creation—including creating us to be God's coworkers and stewards of creation—is a huge act of faith.

Maybe even a gamble. With this much responsibility, if we screw up, it really matters.

My sister—the religious one—loves to make crafts, and she's really good at it. She likes to give them as presents, too. But then she gets so protective of them. She wants to tell you where to hang them or how to use them. To be honest, it drives me a little nuts. But when I think about how much God put into creation, how invested God must be in it working out, it's kind of mind-boggling that God would just give it over to us, entrust us with it.

That might be part of what these early stories about God tell us, too. That God takes risks, that God is actually willing to be vulnerable, which is essentially what it means to be at risk, by sharing the job of caring for creation with us.

It really is hard to imagine. Why do you think God does it?

I think it's in God's nature. God can't help but create, and I think that creating always stems from love.

You mean you can't really create something wonderful because you have to, but because you want to, because you love to do it?

Right. Like we said, one of the most common things the Bible says about God is that God is love. And so I think that God can't help but create out of love. That means sharing creation with us out of love, and taking the kind of gamble we're talking about also out of love.

Maybe that's what it means that we're created, as the first story says, "in the image of God."

What do you mean?

Well, that's one of the famous parts of the first creation story that we haven't talked about much yet. It comes just before God's command to the humans to be fruitful.

Then God said, "Let us make humankind in our image, according to our likeness; and let them have dominion over the fish of the sea, and over the birds of the air, and over the cattle, and over all the wild animals of the earth, and over every creeping thing that creeps upon the earth." So God created humankind in his image, in the image of God he created them; male and female he created them. (Genesis 1:26-27)

Theologians have debated through the ages what "image of God" means. Does it mean that we're rational, capable of ordering the universe, like God does? Does it mean that we can communicate with others, sharing our deepest selves with each other? Does it mean that we're not just physical, like the rest of creation, but also spiritual and connected to God in this way?

And what do you think?

To be honest, I'm not entirely sure. I guess I always figured it was a little bit of each. But now that we're talking about it, I wonder if being made in the image of God is to have this capacity to create, and share, and risk . . . all out of love. You know what I mean? Not because we have to, but because we want to, because that's what it is to be human, to be in God's image, to love so much you can't help but create, share, and risk.

Creating, sharing, risking, all out of love. That sounds a lot like relationships. Actually, it sounds very much like what we said before—that God cares about relationships, especially the relationship God has with us and the relationship we have with each other and all creation.

So does that mean that being created in the image of God is being created to love, to be in relationship with God, creation, and each other?

How does that sound to you?

I like it, a lot actually. But how can we be sure?

Be sure?

Yeah. I've heard people say so many different things about God—about God being all-powerful, or all-knowing, or holy, or just. How can we really be sure that, at heart, God is love?

We probably can't be *totally* sure; that's often the case in theology. And there certainly are lots of things you can say about God, and about God's power and justice and the rest. But I think at some point you have to choose—not between what's true about God and what's false, but about what's *most* true, about what God is *most* like. And when I pay attention to the details of these stories, I have a feeling that's part of what they're telling us, that God creates out of love and wants us to share and even embody that love. I think that's what being created in the image of God means, and I think it's why God's blessing is so central.

God's blessing?

Yes. Before God entrusts humanity with ordering and caring for creation, God blesses them.

What do you mean?

Well, again and again in the first creation story, each day of creation ends with God recognizing that the work of creation accomplished on that day was "good." Except the last day, when it says, "God saw everything that he had made, and indeed, it was very good."

And that's God's blessing?

Yeah, I think it's more than God simply noticing. I think it's like God the artist stepping back and evaluating the work of art, trying to decide whether it merits completing or whether to start over. And when God sees that this work of art—creation—is good, indeed very good, God is blessing it, affirming that it is good in and of itself. It's not good because of what it does, or even because of who made it. Instead, God has blessed creation with an integrity all its own, a worthiness that is woven right into the very fabric of creation. It's the blessing of a loving parent who says to a child, "You know, you're really wonderful."

That's very cool.

Yes, it is. And then it continues, with God inviting humans into the creative work of caring for creation. I think that's another kind of blessing, blessing us with God's affirmation and trust.

Kind of like God is saying, "This is what I made you for. You can do it. I trust you."

Right.

That's very, very cool. And a great way to begin the story, too.

Like we said earlier, beginnings really matter, because they tell you a lot about what's going to come, about the tone of the story. That's true here, too. Whatever comes next, at least in this moment in the story we know that God is a God of love who cares about relationships, and we know just how pleased God is with creation, how eager God is to bless it. So at the start of the story it's probably worth taking just a moment to admire, and be grateful for, God's blessing, God's original blessing.

"Original blessing"? I've heard of "original sin," but not "original blessing."

We'll talk about original sin, too, but before that comes God's original blessing, and with it comes God's promise to hold on to this good creation, to be committed to helping it flourish, both now and into the future.

Original blessing. Yeah, that really is a good way to start.

Insights and Questions

1st Creation Story   very technical
how God created something
       each day
everything is in place now
   Comes 7th day (rest from set up)
Change from direction of work
   to relationship to God.

2nd Creation - Adam & Eve & choice
       or free will
God is helping us to choose
       wisely

When you create showing love
   then there is hope for
better future.

CHAPTER 3

Missing the Mark

Sin

We've covered a lot of ground already. I think I need a recap.

Sounds good. Why don't you give it a try.

Me?

Sure.

Okay. Let's see. Creation. When the Bible talks about creation, it isn't as interested in *how* the world was created—six days or a blinding instant or over millions of years—but in *who* did the creating, namely, God.

Right.

Even more, it's about *why* God is creating. God is creating out of love, intending to share that love with humans and all creation. I guess you could say God creates so that humans and creation would together embody God's love. God took a huge risk, but that's part of it, too—that God creates, shares, and risks out of love. And all of this is part of what the Bible means when God keeps calling creation "good," and at the end, "very good."

Right again. And . . . ?

And . . . God's *still* creating. God not only created once, but continues to keep everything going and uses us to help out. That's why you called us God's partners, helpers, or even, what was the term?

"Co-creators"?

Right. Co-creators, because God invites us into the process of keeping the good creation going through our work, our relationships, all the stuff we do that makes the world a better place.

Exactly.

Well, I like it. I like it, in part, because it helps me make sense of the biblical stories of creation. I mean, I don't have to pretend the Bible is a science textbook and check my brain at the door and ignore everything we've learned from history and science.

Me too.

But I also like that it gives us something to do, a purpose. After all, it's a pretty huge job God is entrusting to us—taking care of creation, taking care of each other, keeping things running and all that. That's a huge job and a really positive picture of human life.

I think so, too.

And I also like it because it's hopeful—the idea that God isn't done yet, and that God uses us to keep the world going, really helps me have hope during some of the difficult times my friend and dad and others have been having.

I agree, and I'm glad it's helpful.

It really is.
But there's one problem.

Oh, what's that?

Well . . .

Yes?

Well, it just doesn't usually work out that way.

Say more.

Do I really have to? This is where our conversation started. My friend's whole life was completely turned upside down all because some idiot drank too much before driving. And my dad might die way before his time.

So, yes, there's a lot of beauty in creation, but also a lot of pain and suffering.

I know that's true, and I know that watching your dad and your friend struggle has been really hard for you.

And it's not just my problems. I mean, there are definitely times when we're busy taking care of each other and the environment and all that. But there are lots of other times, maybe even way *more* times, when we don't.

Just look at the news on pretty much any given day and you're nearly overwhelmed by images of violence and corruption and things generally running amok. Yes, it's a great world, and at the same time it's also a really messed-up world.

I agree. So you're wondering how we square all this with the "original blessing" we just talked about?

Exactly. I mean, good grief, what went wrong? Why is the world such a mess? Yeah, sure, there's a lot of goodness, but also a lot of evil.

The Christian faith has a word for that.

Really?

Yeah—it's short and sweet, but not very popular.

Hmm.

It's called "Sin."

I was afraid you might say that.

Afraid? How come?

Because, frankly, it's such a bummer word.

Nothing personal, but it's hard not to hear the word and start imagining some Bible-thumping preacher wagging a finger and yelling about how we're all sinners and God's going to send us to hell and all that.

Okay, I get the picture. But what if there was another way to talk about sin?

Another way? You mean like we're not sinners?

Not exactly. I actually do think we're sinners. But I don't think sin was meant so much to be an insult as it was simply to tell us the truth.

The truth? About what?

About ourselves. About the messed-up world you were just describing. About our need for God.

I'm willing to listen, but I have to say I'm a little skeptical.

I can understand that. "Sin" has been used by a lot of Christians to put people down.

Yeah, and most of the time it seems like it's used to put *other* people down. You know, "those sinners," the people who disagree with us, do things differently, or don't go to our church.

I know what you mean. But I don't think that way of talking about sin lines up too well with the God we were just talking about earlier.

What do you mean?

Well, we've been talking about a God so full of love that God wants to create—a universe, a world, and people—to share that love with. But when people go ballistic on sin—making it the ultimate insult or put-down—the God we were talking about pretty much disappears.

I hadn't really thought of that.

It's like the God they imagine sits up in heaven with nothing to do but to keep watch, point out all the bad things we're doing, and make sure no one's having too much fun.

Kind of like a twisted Santa Claus.

What?

Well, when you were talking about God sitting around watching us, it reminded me of the song about Santa Claus. You know, "He knows when you are sleeping, he knows when you're awake. He knows when you've been good or bad, so be *good* for goodness' sake!"

That's pretty good. That's a picture of a God who only cares about what we're doing wrong, when we've been talking about a God who loves and creates and wants us to love and create, too. But I think viewing sin as mostly about blame and shame isn't just out of sync with the way we've been talking about God. I think it's also pretty much out of sync with the Bible, too.

Seriously?

Seriously. The word in the New Testament that we most regularly translate as "sin" actually means "missing the mark."

Like in target practice?

Pretty much. When we sin, we miss the mark; we fall short or stray away from God's will for us and for the world. In short, we fail to realize the vision God has for us, the vision of a good world and good people who love and care for each other. Augustine, a very important leader of the church who lived around 400 CE, shaped a lot of what Christians think about sin. He sometimes talked about sin as a great confusion.

Confusion over what?

SIN IS MISSING THE MARK

Augustine said that God gives us people to love and things to use. And sin is when we confuse these and love things and use each other. It's not all Augustine had to say about sin, but it's another illustration of how we "miss the mark."

Okay, that's somewhat helpful. But what about "original sin"? Earlier you mentioned that we'd get to that, and now I'm curious, because while I'm not exactly sure what it means, I do know it sounds really negative.

Say a little more.

Well, think about it. When you talk about "original sin," everything sounds kind of hopeless, like we were born wrong, or bad, or even evil, that there's nothing good about us.

How does that square with the story of creation we talked about earlier?

That's my point. It doesn't.

No, it doesn't. And I want to be clear that the Bible does not call us evil. There's a big difference between being "sinful"—in the sense of being confused, of missing the mark—and being "evil." We may fall prey to evil thoughts, we may do evil things, but humanity is not evil, unredeemable, undeserving of God's attention and love.

Okay. That's a helpful distinction. But I'd still like to know—what happened to the "original blessing" we were talking about? To humans being created good? Does sin wipe all that out?

That's a great question. Another distinction might be helpful to answer it. That distinction is between the particular sins we commit and our general sinful, or fallen, nature.

Say a little more.

Well, "sin" is a big category. Sometimes it's used in the plural to describe the various things we do against God and each other. We may lie, steal, covet, or kill.

That list sounds familiar.

I wouldn't be surprised. Those are all things that are prohibited in the Ten Commandments.

Oh, right—some of the "thou shalt nots."

Exactly. Most of the laws in the Bible deal with God's expectations for how we will treat each other. And when we go against these expectations, we sin. Some of these are sins of *commission*—doing something wrong to someone else—and some are sins of *omission*—not doing something to help someone else.

Okay, I think I've got it. If I cheat on my taxes, or spread gossip about a friend, or refuse to help someone in need, or lie about being sick so I can take a day off of work, I'm committing *sins*, plural.

Right. But "sin" is also used to describe the general human condition. In this case it's not the plural noun naming the things we've done or not done, but a singular noun, and probably capitalized, "Sin." It names our inability to avoid sinning, either by commission or omission. This second kind of "Sin"—singular and capitalized—is what the term "original sin" is getting at.

So why "original"?

That's also a good question, made a little more complicated by the fact that the phrase "original sin" never actually appears in the Bible.

You're kidding! Then where does it come from?

It's a term theologians came up with to make sense of all the different ways the Bible talks about sin, and it describes our damaged relationship with God, creation, and each other. It gets even more complicated because different Christians have understood original sin differently.

This could get very confusing!

It definitely can. But I think maybe the most common and helpful way Christians use the term *original* sin is to describe the basic condition of fallen humanity that we can't escape. We're all born into this condition, so it comes before any of the various and particular sins we might commit.

So "original sin" deals with the big picture, our essential human nature of being confused, like Augustine said, so we tend to love things and use people.

That's essentially it. Original sin also describes our basic and enduring need for God and God's forgiveness, as much as it describes anything we've done or not done.

That's helpful. But I'm still not sure I understand how this fits together with what we called "original blessing." It still feels like it kind of cancels it out.

Some Christian traditions definitely talk about original sin in a way that seems to nullify, or wipe out, God's original blessing. These traditions talk about humanity as "totally depraved," for instance. But I don't think that's really what the biblical story is saying.

But I thought you said the Bible didn't have anything to say about original sin.

The Bible actually has a lot to say about sin and about the human condition; it just doesn't use the term "original sin" any more than it uses the term "original blessing." Both sin and blessing, though, are there from the beginning.

It sounds like you're saying that humans are both blessed and sinful, both good and bad at the same time?

That's very much what I'm saying. And I think that's what the Bible says, too.

But how can we be both?

Maybe at first it seems like a contradiction. But when you stop to think about it, I don't think it's actually all that hard to imagine. I mean, haven't you ever felt yourself torn between doing something you know is right and doing something you know is wrong?

Sure. More than a few times, if I'm going to be honest.

And that's what the Bible is all about—being honest. The apostle Paul, who wrote many of the letters that make up the New Testament, once said, "I can will what is right, but I cannot do it. For I do not do the good I want, but the evil I do not want is what I do" (Romans 7:18b-19).

I've felt that way, too. It's not a particularly good feeling.

No. But like you said, it *is* honest. And for most of human history, whenever philosophers or theologians or artists talk about human nature, they talk about this complicated but honest picture of human beings as being torn between what's right and wrong, as being both good and bad, or, to put it in the terms we've been using, as being blessed and sinful. I mean, it's even in the history of our country.

Really?

Sure. Think, for a minute, of the Declaration of Independence. What's the heart of that document, the part we all memorized in school?

I actually know this: "We hold these truths to be self-evident, that all men are created equal, that they are endowed by their Creator with certain unalienable Rights; that among these are Life, Liberty, and the pursuit of Happiness."

Good memory!
    So what do you think? Goodness of humanity or sinfulness?

No question: goodness.

Okay, so now think about the U.S. Constitution. Do you remember how that starts?

Sure: "We the People, in order to form a more perfect union, establish justice, and insure . . ." something or other.

"Domestic tranquility."

Right. Thanks. I think that's about all I remember.

No problem. That's enough. Because what, even in those first few words, are the framers of the Constitution acknowledging?

That we don't have a perfect union, or justice, or domestic tranquility and the rest.

Exactly. Which is why we need a constitution that sets up a form of government that's based on . . .

Checks and balances! Different branches of government that make sure no single branch gets too powerful.
    Sorry to interrupt, but I think I get it.

61

No problem; go ahead.

It seems that if the Declaration of Independence stresses humanity's goodness and potential, the Constitution acknowledges that we're also bad, or at least confused, like Augustine said.

Exactly. The Declaration of Independence was very much influenced by the thought of John Locke, a British philosopher who was very optimistic about humanity's ability to learn and grow. The Constitution, on the other hand, was more influenced by another British philosopher, Thomas Hobbes, who is best known for saying that life in the state of nature is "solitary, poor, nasty, brutish, and short."

Quite the optimist!

But that's the point—humans, left to their own devices, don't necessarily choose well or do the right thing, which is why we need constitutional checks and balances to protect us from ourselves and each other. Or, to put it in the language we've been using, our government is based on the assumption that human nature is sinful, so that if any one person or branch of government has too much power, things probably won't go so well.

And so the American story contains both of these biblical themes.

Right. A sense of original blessing, but also an acknowledgment of original sin. Original blessing is important because it's from this that we get a sense of our human dignity and rights—that people are worthwhile and deserve protecting. And original sin is important because it lets us be honest and realistic and actually figure out a way to live together.

Interesting.

And it's not just our government that's set up this way, but also our economic system.

Really?

Sure. Do you remember the movie *Wall Street*?

With Michael Douglas?

Right.

Where he makes the "greed is good" speech?

That's the one.

So you think greed is good? That sounds like an odd thing for you to say. Aren't most Christians against greed?

I wouldn't say that greed is good—but just that greed, human interest, is a part of life. The speech Michael Douglas's character makes is essentially that capitalism works because it takes greed seriously. It finds a productive outlet for greed.

And you think he's right?

Actually, I think he overstates the case pretty significantly. I think I'd say instead that capitalism works because it takes both original blessing and original sin equally seriously.

How so?

Original blessing is the desire to create and flourish—original sin is the desire to get ahead, even at someone else's expense. Over time, economists argue, a system that allows for and regulates competing self-interest will yield something that benefits everyone. You might even go so far as to say that communism was doomed to fail because it didn't factor in original sin. It relies on everyone sharing selflessly.

But capitalism has a lot of problems, too. I mean, look at the mess that can happen when people get too greedy and are willing to do just about anything to make a short-term profit.

Which brings us back to checks and balances. The national debate about how much regulation we should have in our financial markets is another sign that we need to—and regularly do—take human sin seriously.

Okay, so I can see how sin is a valuable concept because it paints an honest, if at times painful, picture of the human condition. But to tell you the truth, I'm still not sure I fully understand it. For instance, where does it come from? And why are we like this in the first place?

That's a great question. To answer it, let's go to the source and see what the Bible has to say about sin.

Sounds like a good idea.

We spent a fair amount of time in the Genesis story to talk about creation.

That's for sure.

Well, we're going to go back there to talk about the human condition as well.

You must really like Genesis.

Well, think about it. Genesis, as we said, is about "the beginning"— the beginning of the world, the beginning of humanity, and the beginning of when things went wrong as well.

Okay, I'm game.

It'll be important to keep one thing in mind, though.

Yes?

That Genesis doesn't set out to offer us a scientific view of the world.

Definitely. That was very helpful when it came to talking about creation.

It'll be helpful again when it comes to talking about sin. Like we've said before, the biblical writers are trying to tell us the truth—not the kind of truth that can be proven in a laboratory, but the deeper kind of truth that we build our lives around.

The truth about who we are and where we're going and what's the meaning of this life we share.

Yes, that's nicely put. That is exactly the kind of truth the Bible, including Genesis, is trying to tell us about.

Okay, I'm ready. Then here we go again: "In the beginning . . ."

Yes. Except that as we noticed before, there are two beginnings, two creation stories.

Right. One that seeks to tell us about the orderliness of the world, and the second that zeroes in on the humans who will live in this world.

Exactly. And it's this second story we're going to spend more time with.

Back to Adam and Eve and the Garden of Eden?

Yes, Adam, Eve, and the serpent.

The serpent? Oh yeah, the one who tempts them. This is the part of the story that people call "the fall." Right? Fall from what, though?

Let's get into the story and we'll see. We'll start at the beginning of chapter 3:

> Now the serpent was more crafty than any other wild animal that the
> LORD God had made. He said to the woman, "Did God say, 'You shall
> not eat from any tree in the garden'?" The woman said to the serpent,
> "We may eat of the fruit of the trees in the garden; but God said, 'You
> shall not eat of the fruit of the tree that is in the middle of the garden, nor
> shall you touch it, or you shall die.'" But the serpent said to the woman,
> "You will not die; for God knows that when you eat of it your eyes will be
> opened and you will be like God, knowing good and evil." So when the
> woman saw that the tree was good for food, and that it was a delight to

the eyes, and that the tree was to be desired to make one wise, she took of its fruit and ate; and she also gave some to her husband, who was with her, and he ate. Then the eyes of both were opened, and they knew that they were naked; and they sewed fig leaves together and made loincloths for themselves. (Genesis 3:1-7)

So this is the story of the "forbidden fruit"? I'm not sure I followed it all.

That's okay. But did you notice what's happening in terms of the plot of the story?

What do you mean?

Well, every good story is essentially set in motion by something going wrong, something that introduces dramatic tension, a crisis that you need to escape or a problem you need to solve.

Like how I probably wouldn't pay to go see a movie about two cops getting on a bus to head off to work.

True enough, but what's your point exactly?

That we don't go see movies where everything is normal; that'd be boring. Something has to go wrong. So we're not going to watch two guys just get on a bus for work. But if they get on a bus, the bus goes over fifty miles an hour, and then they discover that if the bus goes below fifty miles an hour it'll explode . . . Well, that's a movie I'd pay money to see.

Especially if you throw in Keanu Reeves and Sandra Bullock just for fun?

Totally. You, I, and millions of others actually did pay to see *Speed* because it set up a problem we wanted the characters to overcome.

Exactly. And something like that happens here, too. The balance of the story is thrown off, a problem is introduced, and dramatic tension is created.

Yeah, I see what you mean. It's not nearly as dramatic as in *Speed*—there's no bomb! But the serpent tells Eve essentially that God isn't being honest with them, that they can eat the forbidden fruit and not die, and that sets up a problem.

Right. Their problem suddenly is whether or not they can trust God. Up to this point in the story, Adam and Eve have a good relationship—really, the ideal relationship—with God, each other, and creation. They trust each other.

Which is what you said the creation account was about—relationships, with God and with each other.

Right. Then something happens.

The serpent introduces mistrust.
I wonder, though . . .

What?

I wonder if Eve would have even thought about eating the fruit if the serpent hadn't questioned it.

That's a good question. Notice how the serpent begins, not at first by challenging God or even by talking about the fruit, but by asking a seemingly innocent question.

Except that it's not right. I mean, the serpent exaggerates what God said to make it sound ridiculous. God didn't say they couldn't eat anything in the garden. And so Eve corrects the serpent, and by doing so brings up God's command about the fruit.

Which the serpent then challenges.

Setting up mistrust, so that they lose confidence in God. And they start to wonder about their relationship with God.

Exactly. Which is where your question about whether Eve would have even thought about eating the fruit is really interesting. Where Adam and Eve were once apparently content, the serpent introduces uncertainty, and that creates a sense of insecurity. And because of that insecurity, they break God's commandment.

So are you saying that original sin really should be called, what, "original insecurity"?

Something like that. Or at least that before original sin comes original insecurity.

Well, I kind of see what you mean, but . . .

But what?

Well, if original sin seems a little harsh, original insecurity seems a little lame.

Yeah, except that what we do out of our insecurity is often pretty awful.

Maybe, but I have to say that eating an apple—even an apple God told you to leave alone—just doesn't seem that bad to me. It's not like they killed someone.

In terms of a moral act, I think you're right: eating forbidden fruit doesn't seem that bad. But I don't think the story in Genesis is trying to say eating an apple is the worst thing you can do. Instead, I think it's trying to describe, to tell the truth about, the human condition.

And you're saying that our condition is dominated by a sense of insecurity.

Yes. And when we feel insecure, we have a choice to make: either we trust in the relationships around us or we take matters into our own hands.

And so the real issue is whether Adam and Eve trust God, the one who made them and put them in the garden.

Right.

So Genesis is painting a picture of the human condition, a condition of uncertainty and insecurity where we always have a choice between trusting someone for our future or taking matters into our own hands. Is that what you mean?

Pretty much, except that I'd add that it seems like we pretty consistently choose to take matters into our own hands.

How come?

I think it's because we experience trusting someone else as surrendering control, even as becoming dependent on that person. Do you know what I mean? Putting our future in someone else's hands, for most of us, is pretty frightening. What if the other person isn't trustworthy? Or what if it doesn't work out the way I want?

I think I get it. Given the choice between trusting someone else and giving up control *or* taking matters into my own hands and staying in control, I'd rather stay in control.

Right. And when you think about it, that's pretty much what the tree of the knowledge of good and evil is all about.

I'm glad you brought that up. I was wondering what's so bad about knowing the difference between good and evil.

Actually, for the people who wrote the Bible, "good and evil" is sometimes used as a catchphrase for "everything," so it might be about learning to distinguish between good and evil, or it might be about learning everything.

So I still don't see the problem. I mean, what's wrong with wanting to know everything? Isn't that why we send our kids to school?

Probably not much, if we were confident and secure on our own. But that's not the situation. Adam and Eve—like all of us—aren't confident on their own. Like it or not, one of the things that makes us human, as we've been talking about, is that we are inherently insecure. The universe is pretty big and we're pretty small. We don't know where we came from. We don't know where we're going.

Like the Doors' song.

Sorry?

"Riders on the Storm." You know,
Into this house we're born,
Into this world we're thrown
Like a dog without a bone
An actor out alone
Riders on the storm.

Exactly. And in that situation, precisely what we want is knowledge. The ability to *know* for ourselves, to not have to trust anyone, including God. Which is where the issue of knowing specifically the difference between good and evil, right and wrong, gets interesting, because when you know that, you suddenly become judge of all the world.

Whew! No wonder they were tempted. That's a powerful promise.

No kidding. As Genesis says, it's the promise to "be like God."

What do you mean?

What they want is what God has—independence. They're no longer content being God's helpers and co-creators; they want to be like God and not have to trust or depend on anyone else. Which brings us back to original sin—not in the sense that we sin because of what Adam and Eve did, or that we're held accountable for their actions, but rather in the sense that we share the same fallen condition of being uncertain, insecure, confused, and often afraid. So we end up trusting ourselves rather than God.

It seems kind of a shame. I mean, at this point in the story, Adam and Eve have everything they could want—the garden, God, each other. But then they wonder if it's enough, if there's something more.

I think that's what temptation is almost always about—trading what you have right in front of you for the promise of something "better." Martin Luther, the sixteenth-century German reformer, once said that he thought "ideals were from the devil."

Aren't ideals a good thing to have?

I don't think he meant the ideal of being honest, for instance. Instead, he meant always longing for some ideal thing instead of being content with the actual thing in front of us. So think about how many people end relationships because the person they are dating or are married to doesn't live up to their ideal. Luther would say that the actual person in front of you is God's gift to you to love, cherish, and nurture. But when you long for the ideal partner, you can't help but end up despising the actual person God gave you, because he or she just isn't perfect.

So whether it's the perfect partner, or the perfect job, or the perfect house, or whatever, we end up preferring some ideal instead of the real person or thing in front of us.

Right.

Interesting.
Have you ever seen the movie *A Simple Plan*?

No, why?

This just reminds me of it. It's pretty much the Adam and Eve story played out in miniature. A guy living in rural Minnesota is out hunting with some friends when they come across a crashed plane with four million dollars. At first he wants to turn it in, but his friends and his wife urge him to keep it. Well, it's an action-suspense film, so things soon start spinning out of control and end in tragedy. What makes it powerful is that before they found the money, they had good lives and were pretty content. But the idea of what they *might* have, what they could have if they keep the money, eats away at them until their lives don't seem adequate anymore and they start grasping for more. Before long they hurt each other deeply and can't trust each other, let alone be happy with what they once had.

I think that's exactly what's going on here. Adam and Eve no longer value the life God created for them and gave them as a gift, and they no longer trust God to provide them with what they need.

Maybe that's why God told them they couldn't eat from the tree of knowledge in the first place. I keep wondering about what the point of that was, but maybe it was just to remind them that there are limits, even for those created as the pinnacle of God's good creation.

I see what you mean. God's command about the fruit reminds them of their incompleteness, of their need. It's a need that can only be filled through relationship with God, the one who created them and invited them to be co-creators in the naming and taming of all living things—the one who offered them identity, purpose, and mission.

That makes a lot of sense, and I think it's also true of their need for each other. After all, Adam and Eve are created as partners and God placed them in the garden to take care of the animals and world together.

But the serpent tells them they don't really need anyone else. They can have what they already have, and more, on their own. And if they get it, then they won't feel so insecure anymore. It's like part of being human is to have this hole inside of you. You know that you're insufficient, not complete, on your own.

And according to the Bible, it's a God-shaped hole, as God is the only thing that can fill it. But we're tempted to think *things* can—whether it's wealth, or attention, or power, or fame, or a piece of fruit that will give us knowledge of everything.

So all of a sudden Adam and Eve think to themselves, "My goodness, but the hole I have is shaped just like that fruit, and if I eat it I'll never ache with incompleteness again." But that's not what happens.

No. I mean, yes. Once they break God's rule and eat, they know the difference between good and evil and all the other stuff. But it doesn't take away that ache. The hole is still there, just as big and demanding as ever. Plus, now they know they don't trust God. Their newfound knowledge only exposes them as insecure and untrusting.

Is that what the story means by saying "they knew they were naked"? That they were exposed?

I'm not totally sure, though I think that's part of it. I know I don't think the Bible is trying to say there's something wrong with the human body.

After all, it's part of God's good creation.

Right. But now Adam and Eve know themselves to be insecure, uncertain, untrusting, and untrustworthy, and they're ashamed of themselves. This is reflected in being ashamed of their exposure, their nakedness, their own bodies.

Then what happens?

Let's go back to the story:

> They heard the sound of the LORD God walking in the garden at the time
> of the evening breeze, and the man and his wife hid themselves from the
> presence of the LORD God among the trees of the garden. But the LORD
> God called to the man, and said to him, "Where are you?" He said, "I

heard the sound of you in the garden, and I was afraid, because I was naked; and I hid myself." He said, "Who told you that you were naked? Have you eaten from the tree of which I commanded you not to eat?" The man said, "The woman whom you gave to be with me, she gave me fruit from the tree, and I ate." Then the LORD God said to the woman, "What is this that you have done?" The woman said, "The serpent tricked me, and I ate." (Genesis 3:8-13)

Everything goes haywire. Just like in *A Simple Plan*, I might add.

I'll rent the movie. I promise!

But you're right; by chasing the illusion of being independent, of being like God, everything is spoiled. What used to give them joy—being in the presence of God—now terrifies them, and so they go hide.

And once God finds them, they start blaming each other for their problems. Which means that now both relationships—with God and with each other—are ruined.

So by the end of the story they know a lot more—the ability to judge between good and evil and all the rest—but they're still insecure. In fact, now all they can do is use their knowledge to judge and blame each other.

Put that way, it's like the Adam and Eve story is the history of the world written very small.

How so?

Well, think about it. This is pretty much what humans do—what all of us do and have been doing—for all of history: we're insecure, confused, uncertain, and so we figure out who we are in terms of who we're not. "I'm white; you're black." "I'm rich; you're poor." "I'm male; you're female." And so on. We establish our identity on the back of someone else.

That's a powerful way to put it.

It's a powerful—and powerfully true—story. And that's what you mean by "sin"—that we all end up defining ourselves *against* other people instead of accepting who we are in relationship *with* each other?

Yeah, and that if push comes to shove we'd actually prefer to replace God, who always reminds us of our incompleteness, with something we can own and control.

Like?

You tell me. It varies with different people. For some it might be wealth, for others power. For some it might be good looks, or sex, or who knows what.

I get it. Each of us has some idea of what it would be like to be independent, to be like God and not need anyone else. But I bet there are really small ways this works itself out, too.

What do you mean?

Money, sex, power—these are all kinds of what I'd call big temptations. But bullying someone else, or putting people down to make yourself look smarter, or being happy when something bad happens to someone else— there are probably millions of ways we choose to love things we think we can control instead of loving God and the people around us.

I think you're right. But no matter how we do it, it comes back to the same thing: because of our original insecurity, we end up not trusting God and each other and try to take matters into our own hands. And in the process we do a lot of damage to each other, to ourselves, and even to the whole world.

The whole world? You mean because we treat the world as one more "thing" that might help us find security.

Exactly. Think about what we've done to the environment by trying to use it to secure our future, taking it over as something we can own and use as we see fit instead of protecting it as the stewards and shepherds that God called us to be.

Okay, that makes sense. But when you think about it, it seems kind of odd that people would call this "the fall."

How so?

Well, it seems Adam and Eve were climbing upward more than they were falling.

Say more.

They were trying to establish themselves on their own, apart from their relationship with God, even though God is the one who created them and gave them life in the first place. That seems more like trying to reach higher than falling down.

Well put. If it's a fall, it does kind of feel like a fall upward.

Except . . .

Yes?

Except that not everyone can fall upward. I mean, not everyone has the power to establish themselves on the back of other people. A lot of people are victims, not victimizers. Would you say that they are sinful, too? That doesn't seem totally fair.

That's a great question. And a complicated one. But I'll try my best to answer it.

Fair enough.

So far, we've been more or less talking about sin as the condition where we do something to someone else out of our insecurity. But there are certainly people who seem less likely to *do* something to someone else than to have something *done* to them.

Exactly.

Well, what if we go back to Adam and Eve and think about their primary identity at the beginning of the story? Who are they at that point?

They're God's creatures, God's children.

Right, so they have an identity—not one they created on their own, but an identity that has been given to them as a gift.

Okay.

We've talked about sin this way: because of our insecurity, we reject the identity God gives us and seek one out for ourselves, usually at the expense of the people around us.

I'm with you.

That's how theologians have talked about sin for centuries. It's a sin of self-assertion. Recently, though, a number of theologians, and especially female theologians who didn't historically have the same power that men did, have asked whether it is also a sin when we surrender the identity God gives us and accept the identity someone else gives us, even forces on us. In that case, we're also not finding or receiving our identity through our relationship with God. This time it's a sin of self-submission, letting someone else call the shots.

You mean it's a sin to try to be *more* than God creates us to be—God's children—but it's also a sin to be *less* than God created us to be, too?

I think that gets at it.

So the person, for instance, who's a racist and says, "Since I'm such-and-such race I'm superior," is sinning and the person who suffers the racism is also sinning? That doesn't seem right.

There's no question that one of these persons has more power and so is actively sinning. But both persons are caught up in the broken, painful human condition that we're describing as fallen, as sinful.

So we're back to thinking about sin both as particular things we do and as our general condition of broken relationships.

Right. It's kind of like, out of our insecurity and confusion, we create one giant pecking order. Whether we're at the top or bottom of it, at least you have a sense of knowing where everything stands.

Which sounds like it's pretty much the opposite of God's act in creation.

Say a little more.

Well, in creation we said God loves us enough to take a risk on us. God creates us but also shares with us the work of creating. Right?

I'm with you.

God creates and cares about our relationship with God and with each other. But because of our insecurity, we respond with mistrust, and we're too afraid to share, precisely because it's way too big of a risk. So rather than find a sense of completion in our relationships with God and each other, we use each other to try to fill our God-shaped hole, just like Augustine was saying.

That's a great way to put it.

And because of all this, we end up doing some pretty stupid things, like hurting people we care about, or stealing money hoping to get wealthy, or driving drunk and crashing into someone.

Yeah, we do a lot of hurtful things.

You know, I think when sin is described that way, it's suddenly a much more helpful way to make sense of the messed-up world we live in.

Great.

I've still got a question, though.

Fire away.

Well, it sounds like we can't really help committing sins.

Say more.

It sounds like simply by being insecure humans—"like a dog without a bone, an actor out alone"—we're going to miss the mark. We're going to use each other to try to deal with our insecurity; we're going to try to be like God instead of in relationship with God.

I think you're probably right.

So are we free or not?

What do you mean?

If we can't help sinning because of the human condition, then I'm not sure whether or not we really have any choice, any free will. And if we don't, then I don't see how we can be held responsible for what happens.

That's another great—and complicated—question, one that theologians have struggled to understand for centuries.

Well, at least I'm not alone.

Definitely not. Here's the short version: We may have no choice about whether or not we live in a sinful condition—meaning we have no freedom about whether we are part of insecure, fallen humanity. But at the same time, we have tremendous freedom to make all kinds of choices for or against God and God's good will and intentions for creation. Trouble is, we regularly choose to use our free will to sin. Or to put it another way: we may have inherited the sinful condition of Adam and Eve, but we make that inheritance our own regularly, relentlessly, and all too often gladly.

That reminds me a little bit of what you said earlier about the apostle Paul. On the one hand, you can feel like you do the things you don't want to, but on the other it's really you choosing to do them. No one makes you.

I think you're right. And at the same time, we're also caught up in a world that is broken and we have no way of avoiding sin. At one point, Paul writes that "the whole creation groans in anticipation."

What did he mean by that?

That the whole world is caught up in sin and looks forward to being redeemed.

Well, I'm not sure I'd go that far. I mean, how can the whole world sin?

I don't think that's quite what Paul meant. Remember in the creation stories in Genesis, God says the world is good, even very good, but never perfect. So in addition to all the orderliness and beauty in creation that we've talked about, there's also illness and accidents and tragedy.

Which we've also talked about, and experienced, firsthand. So part of what Paul is saying is that the whole world groans to be free of cancer and earthquakes and all the rest.

That's definitely part of it. But I think it's also like what you said before: often it feels like we can't escape sin. On the one hand, we regularly choose things that miss the mark of God's good will for us. On the other hand, it also feels like we can't avoid sinning, even if we try with all of our might.

Say a little more about that.

We said earlier that the world is interdependent. God set it up so that we would be connected to each other and need each other. You see that not only in terms of creation—God creating Adam and Eve to take care of each other and creation—but also when it comes to sin.

I'm not sure I'm following.

Let me try an example. Even though I love my kids and try to be a great influence in their lives—and for the most part I think I am a pretty good influence—I also know I'm a damaging influence in their lives. In the same way, no matter how conscientious I am, it seems like I can't buy anything without having a negative impact on the environment, or on people who work for next to nothing to make the stuff I buy, and so on. The car I drive, the clothes I wear—these choices impact others. I can try to minimize the damage I do, but I can't escape actually doing some real damage.

It feels a little like we're these little gerbils running on a great big "sin" wheel, and no matter how hard we run, we'll never get off.

Some church traditions, following Paul, say, "We're captive to sin and cannot free ourselves."

That sounds a little harsh at first, but I think it's right. It really does capture the difficult nature of our life in this world. I mean, it's not that there isn't joy, and love, and hope, and all kinds of other good things—sort of the way creation was meant to be—but it also describes all the hard parts.

Right.

And there's no way back? No way for us to get back to Eden and restore our relationships with God and each other?

To be honest, I don't think that Genesis is really trying to paint a realistic picture of an ideal, sinless past. I think Genesis is far more interested in the present, in describing the way things really are, in offering a story that explains the way of the world. Not explained in a scientific sense, but explained in the sense of putting it in a larger story of God and the people of God so that we can make sense of our experience of life in this world.

Is that why Eve seems to take the blame in the story of the fall—is the story trying to explain why in this culture women have less power than men? I mean, she's the one portrayed as listening to the serpent, like Adam says.

Actually, they both listen.

Really?

Yeah. It says that "she took of its fruit and ate; and she also gave some to her husband, who was with her, and he ate."

So he's there all along, and he just doesn't say anything? Why in the world not?

Who knows? Maybe he's the strong, silent type. Or maybe you're right and this part of the story is constructed to explain the role women play in ancient cultures. But at its core this story isn't about Eve; it's about all of us.

That's helpful, because it sure seems like we're all caught up in the same cycle of sin. In fact, once you understand sin this way—as not only about account-ability but also about our human condition and need for God—you start see-ing sin everywhere: in politics, in our relationships, in the news and media, in the problems in our neighborhoods and homes.

This might be why more than one person, even though perhaps skeptical of Christianity on the whole, has admitted that the doctrine of "original sin" needs no proving.

I'll say. And you're right; it really does help tell the truth about the human condition—about our problems and need.

So on the whole, it sounds like the Christian idea of "sin" is making more sense.

Absolutely. It's actually turning out to be a pretty helpful concept. But it doesn't really answer the question of *why* people get cancer, I don't think. Or why so many are hurt by poverty or hunger, or end up paralyzed because of someone else's bad choices. But at least it tells the truth about all this. It tells us that even though we may be good people in a good world, we're also confused people who regularly hurt ourselves and each other.

I think you've definitely got it.

That raises an obvious question for me, though.

Yes?

Is there any hope? If we can't get back to Eden, is there any way forward?

That question is exactly what the rest of the biblical story deals with.

That must be one long answer.

As we've seen, it's a pretty complicated problem. But we can simplify a bit. The Bible tells the story of what we might call God's drama of redemption.

Well, the beginning of the story has certainly been dramatic.

Yes, it has. And it will only get more so. The rest of the drama really has two main acts. Both have to do with God's quest to redeem God's good creation.

I'm glad to have a front-row seat.

Insights and Questions

Some knowledge is necessary for
living but even a little bit of
knowledge can make you judgmental.
    ex: don't know person's whole
                    story
There is a hole, a longing,
so what do you fill it with?
    Shopping, drug, alcohol, sex
That longing is a joy that
keeps us moving away from God!
Accepting life as it is and
believing that God is a part
of it
Feeling insecure is NOT the issue
what one does with it and what
does it lead to.
Do we gain advantage
Do we take easy way out
Do we want power, pride, fame
Sin is about telling the truth —
God's restoration to us.
Being insecure -- still have
        wants & we don't depend on
                God!

CHAPTER 4

East of Eden

Covenant, Law, and Community

Okay, so my head's spinning a little from everything we talked about. Maybe I can try again to summarize what we said to see if I'm still tracking.

That sounds like a really good idea.

All right, here goes: "Sin" names the specific bad things we do, but also the essential human condition of being insecure, confused, and untrusting. So with Adam and Eve, the problem isn't that God sets limits on them or that they're incomplete or insufficient. They were, after all, made to be in relationship with God and each other.

Sounds good so far.

The problem is that they mistrust God and seek fulfillment apart from their relationship with God. They end up trying to be like God, even to replace God with the things they think will make them independent. And once they do that, they hurt not only their relationship with God but also their relationships with each other and creation.

Do I have that right?

Just right.

Good. Because I thought that was really interesting—that part of being human is *to be* insufficient. No wonder we're a little insecure. Like we said, it's kind of like having a hole inside of us, what we called a "God-shaped hole." The problem comes in how we try to fill that hole.

Yes. Say more.

Well, we need to try to fill that hole with our relationship with God and each other—dealing with our insufficiency by letting others complete us. But we seek to fill it with all kinds of other things: knowledge, power, wealth, fame, drugs, sex, whatever. Sometimes we use others to get what we think will complete us, and sometimes we allow others to use us. Either way, though, as promising as these things seem to be in the moment, they don't fill the hole, at least not for long. Adam and Eve found that out, too.

I think it's interesting that you used the word "promising." Because it really is like these things make promises to us.

That's right. It reminds me of all the advertising we see on TV. If you just use this laptop or wear these running shoes or drive this car, you'll be fine, complete, whole. And it's just not true. I mean, it might be a really great pair of shoes or a wonderful car, but it's not going to change you or your essential situation. It's not going to fill that hole.

Ah, but it's so alluring.

Which is probably why we keep shopping. Right? Even after we've been disappointed by a particular thing—the great car or new laptop—we still believe the larger promise that we can find some *thing* apart from God to fill that hole. And then we're back to Augustine—loving things and using people.

That's, finally, what the "fallen" or "sinful" human condition is all about—missing the mark because we've been distracted by some false promises.

I think that's just right.

Good. I mean, I know sin is even bigger than this. But it seems like almost everything else we talked about—the pecking orders, the harm we do to ourselves, each other, and the world—all of this stems from that essential confusion of thinking we can overcome our "original insecurity" and insufficiency on our own, apart from God and each other.

I think that's a very fair and clear summary of the wide-ranging conversation we had. Nice job.

Thanks.

You know, it's really amazing how important relationships seem to be in the biblical story so far.

Say a little more.

Well, when we talked about creation, it was mainly about God's desire to create out of love and to share that creation with us out of love, even if meant a risk. Well, that's relationship.

Then we talked about sin, and at heart that is also about relationship, except this time it's about our broken relationships with God, each other, and the world because of our insecurity, confusion, and fear.

I think you're right.

So I'm guessing that if things are going to get back on track, then it's going to involve relationships again.

That's a pretty good guess.

So I'm curious to see how that works. Because when we left things, they were kind of a mess—all of us, and the whole creation, for that matter, captive to sin. I guess I don't really see an easy way out, and I can't imagine the God of love who created everything and everyone being content with the mess we're in. So I can't wait to see what God's going to do.

What *God's* going to do? What about *us*?

Well, I suppose we have a role, too, but it seems like the main action is going to have to come from God. After all, it's God who created and blessed us. It's God who established a relationship with us. We've damaged that relationship. It feels like we're just lost and confused enough that we're not going to be able to do it on our own. So I think that whatever may be expected of us, we'll be looking for a big part of the action to come from God.

I guess we'll just have to wait and find out.

Oh, come on. Tell. What's God going to do? It really is a big mess we're in.

Which is why there will be no quick fix. According to the Bible, in fact, God does a number of things worth spending some time on, and two big things in particular.

Fair enough. So where do we start? Oh, wait, let me guess: Genesis? That seems to be a place we've been spending a lot of time, and you said we were going to talk about theology by tracking the plotline of the Bible.

We will enter back into the biblical story in Genesis, though we'll only stay there for a little bit. What God does next, or the move that God makes, takes up much of the rest of the Old Testament. God establishes a community through covenant and law.

Covenant? What's a covenant? Is that more theological jargon?

Hey, come on, I haven't used that much theological jargon.

Oh no? How about original blessing, original sin, sins of omission and commission?

(Jeepers. Just wait until we get to *incarnation*, *atonement*, and *eschatology*.)

What was that?!

Don't worry, we've got a ways to go before these come up, and there's no need to cross any bridges till we get there. For now, let's get back to covenant, which does indeed have a distinct theological and biblical meaning.

 In short, it's essentially like a contract between two parties. Covenants in the ancient world varied, but usually one party made a promise to another, and the other party agreed to do something in return.

And if either party broke the covenant?

As with contracts today, there were usually consequences.

Okay, so you said God establishes a community. That sounds like relationships again! So how does covenant come in?

We're getting there. We first hear about covenants in Genesis, but covenants are important in the rest of the Old Testament, too.

Great. So do we dip back into Genesis right where we left off?

Yes. But just long enough to say this: When God banishes Adam and Eve from the Garden of Eden, God doesn't take back God's original blessing. In fact, God continues to care for them.

How so?

Three things stand out. First, God doesn't punish them with immediate death. God relents from that ultimate punishment and instead banishes them from the garden. Second, despite their sin, God still provides for them, giving them clothes so that they're not left to fend for themselves. And third, they are still invited to care for creation. Near the beginning of the second creation account, it says that God put the man in the garden "to till it and keep it" (Genesis 2:15). Then, after Adam and Eve have disobeyed God, it says again, "The LORD God sent him forth from the garden of Eden, to till the ground from which he was taken" (Genesis 3:23).

So they're not in the garden anymore, but God continues to provide for them and still involves them in caring for the creation, still gives them a role and purpose.

That's right. There's no question that they've lost something. Life "east of Eden" will not be the same as life in the garden, but they're not going out there all alone.

"East of Eden"?

The end of that part of the story says that God placed a guard at the east end of the garden so mortals could not get back in. Over the years, "east of Eden" has become a phrase used to describe life in less-than-ideal situations.

Got it. So what happens next?

Lots of things, like the story of Adam and Eve's children Cain and Abel, Noah and the ark, and the Tower of Babel. But we're not going to cover these things.

Why not? Those sound like some great stories.

They are good stories, and you can certainly read them for yourself. Remember, the key to good Bible study is just to slow down enough to notice the details.

But for now we're focusing on the major plotline of the Bible, and the next big marker in the story comes some years later. God gets involved in the story in a more active way by approaching a man by the name of Abraham with a pretty incredible promise.

So what constitutes "pretty incredible"?

See for yourself: "Now the LORD said to Abram—"

I thought you said his name was "Abraham."

You're right; I did. God changes his name later in the story. It might be simpler just to call him Abraham all the way through.

Okay, go ahead.

All right, taking it from the top:

> Now the LORD said to Abram, "Go from your country and your kindred and your father's house to the land that I will show you. I will make of you a great nation, and I will bless you, and make your name great, so that you will be a blessing. I will bless those who bless you, and the one who curses you I will curse; and in you all the families of the earth shall be blessed." (Genesis 12:1-3)

So let me get this straight: all God asks this guy to do is to move, and God promises to make him the head of a great nation, make him famous, bless

him, and protect him? That does sound like an incredible offer. Kind of hard
to refuse, actually.

It's a little trickier than that because the new land is really far away,
and he's going to have to cover some dangerous ground to get there.
But that's not all. Abraham's seventy-five years old, and he and his
wife, Sarah—called Sarai here, but her name changes, too—don't
have any children because Sarah has been barren all her life.

She couldn't have children?

Nope. Which makes the promise of a great nation a little dicey,
right?

No kidding. That changes things more than a little. What does he do?

He picks up and leaves. He heads for the land God told him to go to.

Really? Good for him. And how does it turn out?

He makes it to the promised land, though not without some inci-
dents—again, definitely worth your reading at some point. But then
he's there for another fifteen years and nothing happens—no child,
nothing.

So what gives? Has God forgotten?

No, though at times Abraham believes that God has. At long last,
though, God comes and renews the promise to Abraham and makes
a covenant with him. And it's at the making of the covenant, actually,
that God changes Abraham's name.

Why?

To signify the promise God makes. As we've already seen, names in
the Bible often tell something important about the persons who bear
them.

**Like "Adam" really means "the one who came from the earth" and "Eve"
means "living."**

Right.

So what does "Abraham" mean?

"Abram," his original name, means "exalted ancestor."

That's not bad.

Not at all. But "Abraham" means "ancestor of a multitude."

Ah, I see. It really does capture the heart of God's promise.

But that raises a question for me: Why does God make this covenant in the first place? I mean, God is God, but who are humans to demand a contractual agreement from God? It seems like that's a little much to expect.

That's a fair point. Truth be told, humans could not ask or expect a covenant from God, and in the story they don't. God actually initiates all the covenants in the Bible and chooses freely to enter into them.

Covenants, plural? Just how many covenants did God make?

Four major ones.

Four? What's wrong with the one God made to Abraham? Why make three more?

That gets to the heart of the question you asked just a moment ago: Why does God make covenants in the first place? I think the answer has to do with your earlier observation about how important relationships are to God.

In what way?

Well, think about the power of promises for a minute. You know what I mean? Promises create something; they call something into being by drawing the one making the promise and the one receiving the promise together. When I tell my kids that we'll go sledding as soon as I'm home from work, it affects both of us. I certainly make sure I can get done with work on time and be home to keep my promise, but they also make sure everything is ready to go when I get there. The promise draws us together in this kind of shared expectation about the future.

You think that's why God makes covenants?

Very much so. Like you said, God doesn't have to do this. And, like you also said, God is all about relationships. And what better way to establish and strengthen a relationship than through a promise?

Plus, the covenant is a public promise; it's a serious deal. A marriage ceremony, which involves exchanging of vows and promises, is something like a covenant. It's a promise, for sure, but it's also made publicly and takes the relationship to a new level.

So the covenant is for Abraham's sake?

I think so. Covenant becomes a way for God to reestablish a relationship with people. In this sense, you were right: God is the one who takes the initiative to draw sinful human beings back into relationship with God, in this case by establishing a relationship with Abraham and, just as importantly, with all his descendants. Over the years, the covenant will remind them again and again of God's promises. It will create and nurture in them an identity as the children of God, and it will draw them closer to God in this future expectation.

You mentioned Abraham's descendants. So I gather he and Sarah do have children and also that the promise is bigger than Abraham, even if he's the one receiving it.

They have one child, named Isaac.

Just out of curiosity, what does "Isaac" mean?

"Child of laughter." When Sarah overhears God tell Abraham that she's going to have a baby at age ninety, she begins to laugh.

I guess I can't blame her. I think I'd laugh, too, or maybe cry. Ninety! Wow!

No doubt. But, yes, they have descendants and, yes, the promise is bigger, way bigger, than just Abraham.

What do you mean?

That God isn't only creating a relationship with Abraham through the covenant. God is creating a community, and through this community God intends to restore relationship with the whole world.

Really?

Really. It's right there in that original promise we heard: "In you all the families of the earth shall be blessed" (Genesis 12:3b).

I missed that the first time.

It's easy to do. We tend to think of blessings as something really cool—and of course they are—but we tend to think about them kind of personally, even privately. But in the Bible, anytime God blesses you, it's so that you can be a blessing to someone else.

Blessed to be a blessing. Interesting . . .

What?

It occurs to me that the politicians are only getting it half right.

How do you mean?

Well, politicians usually end their speeches these days by saying, "God bless America." Which is fine, of course. There's no question God has blessed America in all kinds of ways. But it seems that, if they're talking about the biblical God, they should probably say, "God bless America, so that America can be a blessing to the world."

That's an excellent point.

You said God makes four major covenants. Are we going to cover the other three?

Yes, though not all in the same detail.

The first covenant God makes is way before Abraham. It's made to Noah and his children after the flood. God promises not to destroy the world by flood again. Not ever.

Thank goodness!

No kidding. It's a pretty straightforward one, so we're not going to spend a lot of time with that one.

The second covenant is the one with Abraham, which we've been talking about, and it's the promise of land and descendants.

The fourth covenant is one that God makes with David. David is a king in Israel, and he's widely considered the greatest of Israel's kings.

What's the covenant that God makes to David?

That one of his descendants will always be the king of Israel.

Not bad.

But you skipped one? What happened to the third covenant?

That's where we'll go next, to talk about Moses and the covenant that God makes with the Hebrew people at Mount Sinai after leading them out of Egypt.

God entered into four covenants with the people of Israel

Noah	Abraham	Moses	David
No more flood to destroy earth	Descendants Land Blessing	The Law at Mount Sinai	Family of Kings forever

Oh, good. I love that story and have seen both the original Charlton Heston movie and *The Prince of Egypt*. But now that I think about it, I'm not sure I know how Abraham's descendants . . . because that's who the Hebrew people are, right? . . .

Yup.

. . . how Abraham's descendants got to Egypt in the first place.

It's a long story and, again, well worth your time to read for yourself. But essentially they traveled there during a severe famine when one of Abraham's great-grandchildren, Joseph, worked for the pharaoh of Egypt. Years later, though, the descendants of Abraham have grown in number and the Egyptians begin to get worried that they're getting too big, that they might side with one of Egypt's enemies and try to take over Egypt. So the Egyptians make them slaves and treat them increasingly harshly.

Is there any sign that the people were conspiring against the Egyptians, or is this one more example of how the usual human tendency to insecurity and fear leads to violence?

Pretty much the latter.

In any event, it's here that Moses enters the picture.

Right. I remember that he's actually raised in Pharaoh's home, but then he has to run away because he kills a guard who's abusing one of the Israelites. Later God appoints him as the one to confront Pharaoh and bring the Israelites out of Egypt.

It's a really great story.

It really is, and it contains two of the high points of Israel's history.

The rescue from Egypt has to be one.

Right. And the other is the giving of the law at Mount Sinai.

Of course. That's why the whole movie is called *The Ten Commandments*.

Exactly. And it's in the giving of the law that God renews God's covenant with Israel.

Or, I should probably say that God renews the covenant with Israel, and then gives the people the law.

What's the difference?

Well, there are two choices at this point. Either God gave Israel the law to help Israel *become* God's people. Or God gave Israel the law because Israel *already is* God's people. In the first case the law is primarily the instrument needed *to win* God's favor; in the second it's *the sign* of God's favor.

What does the Bible say?

It's a little ambiguous at this point. Here's the main part of the story, where God speaks to the Israelites from Mount Sinai after God has brought them up out of Egypt:

> *Then Moses went up to God; the LORD called to him from the mountain, saying, "Thus you shall say to the house of Jacob, and tell the Israelites: You have seen what I did to the Egyptians, and how I bore you on eagles" wings*

*and brought you to myself. Now therefore, if you obey my voice and keep
my covenant, you shall be my treasured possession out of all the peoples.
Indeed, the whole earth is mine, but you shall be for me a priestly kingdom
and a holy nation. These are the words that you shall speak to the Israel
ites." So Moses came, summoned the elders of the people, and set before
them all these words that the* LORD *had commanded him. The people
all answered as one: "Everything that the* LORD *has spoken we will do."*
(Exodus 19:3-8a)

Treasured possession. That's nice.
Okay, so is this before God gives the law or after?

Before. The giving of the law comes next.

**I see what you mean. On the one hand, God establishes the covenant and
after the covenant is made, God gives the law. So it's not like the law is the
way to become God's people. At this point in the story, they already are God's
people.**
**At the same time, it sure sounds like the people have something to do:
they need to obey God's voice and keep the covenant.**
So what do you think?

I think that Israel obeying God's voice, keeping the commandments
God is about to give, is really important. But on the whole, I think the
law is not primarily an instruction manual on how to win God's love.
Instead, I think it's the instruction manual that God gives because
God *already* loves Israel. It's an instruction manual for getting the
most out of life, for living in a new land as a free people.

I'm not sure I understand.

Keep in mind that the Israelites have been slaves in Egypt for generations. When Moses first came to them and said that God was going
to rescue them, they couldn't even believe it because of, as the Bible
says, "their broken spirit and cruel slavery" (Exodus 6:9). So God
gives them the law to help them live as free people. But the covenant
made through Moses with the Israelites is really a renewal of the covenant God had already made with Abraham.

So it's not completely new?

No, and that's another reason that I think the law is a gift *to* God's people rather than the means to *become* God's people. The covenant made at Sinai may be extended to the whole nation, but it's essentially renewing and expanding the covenant God already made to Abraham and his descendants. Here's how the Bible describes it:

> God also spoke to Moses and said to him: "I am the LORD. I appeared to Abraham, Isaac, and Jacob as God Almighty, but by my name 'The LORD' I did not make myself known to them. I also established my covenant with them, to give them the land of Canaan, the land in which they resided as aliens. I have also heard the groaning of the Israelites whom the Egyptians are holding as slaves, and I have remembered my covenant. Say therefore to the Israelites, 'I am the LORD, and I will free you from the burdens of the Egyptians and deliver you from slavery to them. I will redeem you with an outstretched arm and with mighty acts of judgment. I will take you as my people, and I will be your God. You shall know that I am the LORD your God, who has freed you from the burdens of the Egyptians. I will bring you into the land that I swore to give to Abraham, Isaac, and Jacob; I will give it to you for a possession. I am the LORD'." (Exodus 6:2-8)

I see what you mean. It's pretty clear that God is rescuing the Israelites as part of keeping God's promise to Abraham.

I'm not sure I follow that part about God's name, though.

Can you say more?

Well, the name God used with Abraham was "God Almighty." Right? But here in this part of the Bible, God wants to be known as "The LORD." What's up with that?

That's a pretty interesting part of the story. Once again, it has to do with the power of names.

You mean like with Adam, Eve, and Abraham; their names all tell something deeply true about them.

Right, but names don't only *describe* in biblical times, they also *reveal* something about a person's character. Which makes names pretty powerful. If someone's name reveals something about his or her character—something about who they are—then you've got something of

96

a hold on that person. He or she can't really fool you, you know what I mean? It's like when one person says to another, "I *know* you. You can't get away with that."

I think I know what you mean, but I'm not following how this fits into the story.

We have to go back just a little, to when Moses first encounters God in the burning bush.

Sure, I remember that from the movies, too. Isn't that where Moses first hears that God has heard the cries of the people and plans to rescue them?

Right, and God also says that he's going to send Moses to be the one to do it.

Oh yeah, and Moses isn't all that excited about going back to Egypt, because he doesn't know if Pharaoh wants him dead, or even how the Israelites will receive him.

Which is presumably why Moses asks God for something of a calling card:

> But Moses said to God, "If I come to the Israelites and say to them, 'The God of your ancestors has sent me to you,' and they ask me, 'What is his name?' what shall I say to them?" God said to Moses, "I AM WHO I AM." He said further, "Thus you shall say to the Israelites, 'I AM has sent me to you.'" God also said to Moses, "Thus you shall say to the Israelites, 'The LORD, the God of your ancestors, the God of Abraham, Isaac, and the God of Jacob, has sent me to you.' This is my name for ever, and this my title for all generations." (Exodus 3:13-15)

What's up with the "I am"? I mean, what kind of name is that?

Here's where the thing about names becomes important again. Think about Moses' situation. He fled Egypt, but now he's married and has a comfortable life. Then, out of the blue, this burning bush starts talking to him. He knows this is extraordinary, holy, and probably a little dangerous. He's being drawn into conversation with the God of his ancestors. But then things get even more exciting.

Or worse, depending on your point of view.

Or worse. That's right. Because God tells Moses to go back to a powerful ruler who wants him dead, and to a people who aren't too wild about him either.

On the other side of the equation, though, God has promised to deliver the people from their oppression and bring them to the promised land.

Which means that the question before Moses is . . .

Whether he can trust God.

Interesting. It comes down to trust again, trust in a situation of uncertainty, insecurity, and fear. Just like Adam and Eve. And just like Abraham, too, now that I think of it. God asks something extraordinary of Abraham, and he trusts God.

He does, though not all the time. We didn't get into that part of the story, but Abraham also has his moments of not trusting. But you're right: when you're talking about relationships, you're always talking, on one level or another, about trust.

So when Moses asks for God's name, there's actually more going on than asking for a calling card. It's kind of a power play.

Exactly. Moses wants God to reveal something of God's own character, to give Moses a bit of a handle on God so Moses doesn't feel quite so out-there, all alone. After all, Moses is being asked to trust God, this God he has just been introduced to.

And then God goes and says, "I am who I am."

The verbs have a future sense to them, so you could actually translate it, "I will be who I will be."

Beautiful. It's as if God is saying, "Don't box me in, Moses. You want to know who I am? I'll tell you who I am: 'I AM WHO I AM.' How do you like them apples?!"

Kind of an in-your-face answer when you think about it that way.

That's exactly right. God won't be pinned down. God enters into relationships freely, because God wants to, because it's in God's nature to make promises and to keep them. But you can't force God to be and do what you want.

And how does Moses take all this?

Moses goes along with it, though a little reluctantly. God sends Moses' brother Aaron with him, so he's not all alone, and that helps. You've seen the movie, so you know the rest. God rescues the Hebrew people—who later will become the ancient Israelites—from Pharaoh and brings them out of Egypt. In the end, Moses comes to know who the LORD is by witnessing what the LORD does.

Which is maybe why God begins the covenant renewal by reminding them of what God already *did*: "I bore you on eagles' wings and brought you to myself. Now, therefore, . . . "

I think you're right. God knows how hard it is to trust, so God reminds the people that they have good reason to trust God because of everything God has done. God has kept the promise, the covenant God had already made with Abraham. And now God is renewing and extending it.

Which brings us back to the law. It's God's *gift* to those who already are God's people, whom God has already treated as God's treasured possession.

Exactly. And noting that difference—that the law is a gift to God's people, not the means by which to become God's people—makes a huge difference in how you understand the law.

In what way?

If you think the law is something you use or obey in order to earn or keep God's favor, then the law is primarily about God, about keeping God happy. But if you think the law is a gift because you're already God's people, then the law is primarily about you, about keeping you safe and helping you get the most out of life.

I think kids sometimes confuse this. At least, I know I did when I was a kid. Whenever my parents made rules, I assumed they did it just because they could, kind of like tyrants. But when I think about it, most of the rules they made were essentially about keeping me and my siblings safe. You know, "Don't play in the street." "Be home on time." "Get your homework done." It wasn't about making them happy; it was about helping us get the most out of life.

The Ten Commandments are very much like that. We may think about them a little negatively because of all the "you shall not" phrases, but they're really about how to get the most out of life now that the Israelites are free people.

And they're also pretty general, if I remember.

Let's look at them in more detail:

> *Then God spoke all these words:*
> *I am the LORD your God, who brought you out of the land of Egypt, out of the house of slavery; you shall have no other gods before me.*
> *You shall not make for yourself an idol, whether in the form of anything that is in heaven above, or that is on the earth beneath, or that is in the water under the earth. You shall not bow down to them or worship them; for I the LORD your God am a jealous God, punishing children for the iniquity of parents, to the third and the fourth generation of those who reject me, but showing steadfast love to the thousandth generation of those who love me and keep my commandments.*

*You shall not make wrongful use of the name of the L*ORD *your God, for the L*ORD *will not acquit anyone who misuses his name.*

*Remember the sabbath day, and keep it holy. Six days you shall labor and do all your work. But the seventh day is a sabbath to the L*ORD *your God; you shall not do any work—you, your son or your daughter, your male or female slave, your livestock, or the alien resident in your towns. For in six days the L*ORD *made heaven and earth, the sea, and all that is in them, but rested the seventh day; therefore the L*ORD *blessed the sabbath day and consecrated it.*

*Honor your father and your mother, so that your days may be long in the land that the L*ORD *your God is giving you.*

You shall not murder.

You shall not commit adultery.

You shall not steal.

You shall not bear false witness against your neighbor.

You shall not covet your neighbor's house; you shall not covet your neighbor's wife, or male or female slave, or ox, or donkey, or anything that belongs to your neighbor. (Exodus 20:1-17)

Don't murder. Don't steal. Don't commit adultery. Don't lie. And so forth. Not exactly rocket science.

That's right. The Ten Commandments lay down basic parameters of life for free people. Essentially, they are about treating each other with respect, treating each other the way you'd want to be treated, not like you were treated when you were slaves. These are the kinds of things you need to agree to if you're going to live with each other peacefully.

I think I see something else, though.

Okay. Shoot.

It seems like the Ten Commandments really go in two basic directions.

What do you mean?

Well, it's like what we've been talking about all along. The first couple of commandments are about our relationship with God, and the rest are about our relationship with each other.

That's a helpful observation. God's law, along with the covenant, is a primary way God seeks to draw us back into relationship, both with God and with each other. At one point in the Gospels, someone asks Jesus what the most important law is, and he says essentially the same thing:

> "You shall love the Lord your God with all your heart, and with all your soul, and with all your mind." This is the greatest and first commandment. And a second is like it: "You shall love your neighbor as yourself." On these two commandments hang all the law and the prophets. (Matthew 22:37-40)

Yeah, there it is again.

But aren't there tons of other laws in the Bible? Like some really strange ones, and lots that talk about putting people to death when they don't obey the law?

When reading Israel's laws, it's really important to distinguish between two kinds of law: *absolute law*, which is the same in all times and places, and *conditional law*—sometimes called "case law"—which applies only in certain situations.

"You shall not kill" sounds pretty absolute.

Exactly right. The Ten Commandments, which are the absolute law of Israel, apply in all situations. Most of the rest of the laws in the Old Testament are case law. For instance, "When an ox gores a man or a woman to death, the ox shall be stoned, and its flesh shall not be eaten; but the owner of the ox shall not be liable" (Exodus 21:28).

I see what you mean. This isn't something you and I are likely to run into that often.

Right. The conditional or case laws are Israel's attempt to apply the absolute law to the varied situations they will find themselves in.

But doesn't Israel credit God for all of their laws?

Yes, they do, and that's important for two reasons. First, you can see case law change over time, so there's no question that as the Israelites' situation changes, so does their sense of how best to apply the heart of the law to their situation. Second, they are right in saying that all of their laws come from God. Why? Because in doing so they are confessing just how much God loves them, how much God wants to be in relationship with them and for them to be in relationship with each other. And that law is, along with covenant, the way God maintains that relationship.

Say a little more about that.

What's really astounding about the Ten Commandments isn't their content. As we've already noticed, they're kind of common sense. And, for that matter, there are other ancient law codes with similar instructions. What's incredible about the Ten Commandments is that God gives them to Israel out of love. The same God who rescued them from Egypt is now setting them up for life in the land by giving them these laws to live by.

Like parents do.

Exactly. So every time the Israelites try to apply this law to their particular circumstances, they can and should give credit for the attempt to the God, because they are continuing to try to extend God's concern for them, for others, and for creation.

For others and for creation?

Sure, take the commandment about the Sabbath, for instance. We tend to think about it as a command about worshiping God—like, "You can't do anything on Sunday because that's *my* day."

Yeah, I'd say that's pretty much the way I grew up with it and the way, I think, my sister still treats it.

But look more carefully at what the commandment actually says:

> *Remember the sabbath day, and keep it holy. Six days you shall labor and do all your work. But the seventh day is a sabbath to the LORD your God; you shall not do any work—you, your son or your daughter, your male or female slave, your livestock, or the alien resident in your towns. For in six days the LORD made heaven and earth, the sea, and all that is in them, but rested the seventh day; therefore the LORD blessed the sabbath day and consecrated it.* (Exodus 20:8-11)

So it's not about God; it's about rest. And not just rest for a few people, but for everyone, from the highest to the lowest, including your animals.

That's right. There's clearly a sense of remembering God and how God created the world, but the force of the commandment is so that everyone has a chance to rest and be renewed, just as God did.

That puts a whole other spin on the law. That it's not primarily even about us, as individuals, but about the whole community.

Biblical law is always about your neighbor, about the persons around you, about the larger community, rather than just about you.

That makes a lot of sense, once you get used to it. I mean, maybe at first it doesn't sound all that great having to worry about your neighbor all the time, until you remember that all your neighbors are also worrying about you.

I have to say, though, that this sounds a little different than many of the "Christian" books I see in bookstores. You know, the ones that are always about "your best life now." They seem like the Christian faith is primarily about getting a great big house, or lots of money, or a really cool car.

You're right. That's definitely a far cry from what we're discovering in the biblical story, where we're regularly instructed to work for our *neighbor's* best life, rather than our own.

You know, it's interesting. I keep thinking about how much this all sounds like the rules parents make for their kids, like we said before. What I think most of us didn't understand when we were kids was that our parents didn't care so much about the rules. What they really cared about was us. They were worried that if we didn't follow their rules we'd miss out, get hurt, or hurt each other.

I think you're right.

It actually reminds me of something that happened to me as a kid. It's a little embarrassing, but I think it captures what we're talking about.

I'd love to hear it.

Okay, so one time when I was eight or nine, I got into this argument with my little brother, and before long arguing turned into pushing and shoving, and then pushing and shoving turned into hitting. And then all of a sudden

my mom was there, just as I had my brother pinned down and was about to smack him good.

Uh-oh.

No kidding. She hollered across the room for me to stop it immediately.

And what did you do?

You're not going to believe it, but I just looked at her, point blank, and then said that since this was my little brother, I could do whatever I wanted with him.

Actually, I've got a ten-year-old at home, so I do believe it. And what did your mother do?

She swooped across the room, towered over me, and bellowed, "He's MY son—NO, YOU CAN'T!"

I think that's what's behind the force of all the "thou shalt nots" we talked about. God is saying something like, "They're my children—all of them—so, no, you can't murder them, lie to them, betray them. No, you can't have everything, hoard everything, keep everything."

You know what I mean? All of the people God created are God's treasured possession, and so ultimately God wants to be in relationship with all of them. That's why God gives the law.

I think you're absolutely right. God forms a community with Abraham and his descendants through both covenant and law and in this way reestablishes the relationship that was damaged in Eden. But it goes beyond this, too. I think God's actually trying to reach out not only to Abraham's descendants but to all the world.

I'm not sure I follow.

In establishing the covenant with Abraham, and then with Moses, and then with David, God is building a people that God wants to be different from the world of "What have you done for me lately?" and "You've got to look out for number one." God wants Israel to be an example of a different kind of community, to model a different way of living in the world. And so while Israel adopts all kinds of customs to set themselves apart—from the kind of food they'll eat to the clothes they wear—what really sets them apart is obeying a set of laws that treat people like they really are God's children.

In this way, they really do carry God's original blessing, like they really do have dignity and worth in and of themselves. And they obey these laws because they reflect God's covenantal promise to be in relationship with them no matter what. I think the hope is that the other nations will see this different community, this different way of living in the world, and want to be part of it, too.

Covenant, law, and community, all to be a blessing for the whole world. I have to say that I think it's a pretty cool idea. How does it all work out?

Sometimes pretty well, sometimes not. Most of the Old Testament, in fact, tells the tempestuous story of Israel trying, and regularly failing, to keep the law, to honor God's wishes.

The story of Israel missing the mark.

Again and again and again. But the story always tells of God running after Israel, sometimes in warning, sometimes in judgment, sometimes in comfort and healing, but always trying to draw Israel more deeply into that covenantal relationship and through that relationship to bless the whole world.

How does God go about doing that, drawing Israel back into relationship?

It's a long and sometimes complicated story, and definitely worth reading! But in brief, God regularly reaches out to Israel through judges, kings, and prophets in order to draw them back into relationship.

Whoa. I know we can't go into the whole story, but you're going to need to slow down just a bit. What's a judge?

Something like a tribal elder, someone appointed to defend Israel from enemies and to hold Israel accountable for following God's law. For a long time, Israel isn't so much a nation as it is an alliance of the twelve tribes that make up Abraham's descendants. There's a book in the Old Testament called Judges that tells the story of this part of Israel's history.

I can guess what a king is, and I'm assuming this is where David comes in.

That's right. David is the second king of Israel, and this is when the descendants of Abraham really become a nation. Their job is similar to that of the judges, but it's on a much bigger scale and far more formal. You can read about the formation of Israel as a nation and the story of its kings in the books of 1 and 2 Samuel, 1 and 2 Kings, and 1 and 2 Chronicles.

And the prophets?

The prophets are the spokespeople for God. You can read about them in the books that bear their names. Isaiah, Jeremiah, and Ezekiel are the major figures, and then there are a host of minor prophets as well.

The primary job of the prophets was to call the people back into the two primary relationships we've been talking about, relationship with God and relationship with each other and creation. Except that, for the prophets, sometimes it's hard to distinguish between the two.

What do you mean?

Just that for the prophets, it's nearly impossible to talk about being in a good relationship with God if you're ignoring or abusing your neighbor. The two go together.

That makes sense.

So for good or ill, the prophets regularly have a clear vision of what God wants for Israel and how God wants Israel to live.

For good or ill? How can that be bad?

Maybe it's not bad for the people, but it's often very hard for the prophets.

How come?

Because when the king or the nation is making a mess of God's law, the guy to come and tell you to straighten up usually isn't that popular. Even more, it can be pretty painful for the prophets to see how far Israel strays from keeping God's law. They have to witness how much pain and suffering Israel brings on itself and how much joy and love they miss out on.

Because that's what God feels. Again, it's like a parent who loves her child so much she just can't help but feel everything her child feels.

Like we said, parental imagery is very common in the Bible. And there's other imagery like that, too, especially in the prophets. That's where God is sometimes described as a judge, sometimes as a betrayed spouse, sometimes as a shepherd, and sometimes as a lover. The prophets tried just about every image they could think of to convey how desperately God wants to be in relationship with Israel and with the world through Israel.

And whenever you want something that much, you're really vulnerable and feel the disappointment deeply. It can be really hard to love someone that much.

Very hard. Near the end of the Old Testament story, in fact, the prophets begin wondering whether it can possibly all work out.

Do they think God is giving up on them?

No. They know relationships—all relationships, including the one we have with God—are filled with ups and downs, which is why forgiveness is so important.

Say a little more.

In time, we'll have a lot more to say. But for now, it's probably enough to say that it's clear from both the Bible and our daily lives that over the long haul you just can't keep score in a relationship, or it will kill you. You know what I mean—keeping tabs on every slight, every injury . . .

I've known people like that—they're miserable . . . and lonely.

Right, and so forgiveness is essentially wiping the scoreboard clean, starting over.

And that's part of the Old Testament story, too?

All over the place. Sometimes there are rituals and sacrifices that accompany the forgiveness; sometimes it just comes as God's pronouncement and promise. But it's always there for Israel, and it makes continuing in the covenant possible.

But the prophets still aren't sure it's all going to work out?

After a while, they begin wondering whether covenant and law are enough to form a new and lasting community, and so they talk about God doing a completely new thing (Isaiah 43:18-19). In time, they begin looking forward to God making a new kind of covenant altogether, one not written on paper but on people's hearts (Jeremiah 31:31-34). By the end of the story that the Old Testament tells, the prophets will look for God to send a new kind of prophet and king—a messiah—who's going to save them not just from the Egyptians, but from all the people who will try to oppress them and, ultimately and perhaps especially, from themselves.

And is that where Jesus comes in?

Yup, that's where Jesus comes in.

I was wondering when we'd get to him.

I think we're there now.

Good. I'm very interested to see what happens.

Insights and Questions

God said " I am who I am " Don't put God in a box.

God gave 4 covenants because people tried & failed. God didn't give up on them. He saw some improvements but he also knew Israelites needed more help.

God gave 10 commandments (the laws) because he loved the people and showed them how to live life and to live in freedom.

When the time was right Jesus was able to come because enough people were able to understand who God was

Because of human sin God doesn't abandon us but he answers our prayers in his way & in his time.

God's command - Live as free people in relationship with one another

The intent of the law -- love God & love your neighbor. He is trying to make relationships work. Covenant is a promise of God & man. our side is flawed.

CHAPTER 5

God con Carne

Incarnation

So, it's on to Jesus.

That's the idea.

I guess we're going to talk about his cross and resurrection?

We certainly will, but first we're going to start with his birth.

Really? Christmas? I mean, his birth is what Christmas celebrates, right?

That's right.

Christmas, actually, is the one holiday we can celebrate in my family in relative peace. What's to fight about? Who can get upset about a baby? We'll even go to church together sometimes. Even my brother comes. It's nice with the candles and carols, and we enjoy giving each other gifts.

I think a lot of families celebrate Christmas that way. But you sound a little surprised.

I guess it makes sense to start here since we're following the biblical plotline. Jesus has to be born before he can do anything else. But I'm not sure how Christmas will help answer my questions about my friend and dad, about why there's so much suffering in the world and what God's going to do about it.

> Would you be surprised if I said that the early Christians discussed, argued, and fought over what we celebrate at Christmas more than any other thing in the history of Christianity?

You've got to be kidding!

> No. For most of the third and fourth centuries, the early Christians debated what we now sing about in our Christmas carols with candles glowing all around us.

That Jesus was born in a manger?

> Yes. But specifically that, in Jesus, God became human.

Hmm. I think that's something I probably haven't thought about too much, to be honest. I know we call Jesus the Son of God, but I'm not sure I've thought about how Jesus can be both human and God at the same time. Or how God can be in heaven and on earth in Jesus at the same time. Or what you even mean when you say God became human.

> Those are exactly the questions the early Christians were asking.

And this will help answer some of my questions? I realize that maybe there aren't complete answers, and I know that our discussion about sin helped describe the fallen world we live in, where people die of cancer and car accidents all the time, but I'd still like to hear more about how God is taking care of all this.

> We've also talked about how God is at work continuing the creative activity of caring for the world through us, which is good to remember, too. But why don't we look at what Christians have said that God is up to in Jesus, and then see how this addresses your questions?

Sure, I'm willing to see how this plays out. But I've got one other question first, if that's okay.

> Absolutely. Please go ahead.

Thanks, because I'd like to go back, for a minute, to where we left off with covenant, law, and community.

Okay.

Well, it seems like a good plan. God chooses Israel, starting with Abraham, and through them blesses the whole world. Lots of potential there.

The authors of the Old Testament thought so, too. So what's the question?

Well, what happened?

What do you mean?

I guess I'm wondering whether the plan failed.

Could you say a little more? I'm not following.

You know, the plan to restore relationship with humanity and bless the whole world through the covenant God made with Israel. I'm wondering if it failed. I mean, it became clear through our conversation that the ancient Israelites struggled a lot with holding up their end of the agreement. That's why the judges, kings, and prophets got involved.

Yes, it was definitely a bumpy road at times.

Like you said, though, that's true of most relationships. But if God goes and does a new thing with Jesus, then it feels like one of two things must have happened.

Yes?

Either the original plan with Israel failed and Jesus is part of plan B, or Jesus was part of the plan all along.

What do you think?

I'm really stuck. On the one hand, if the plan failed, you have to wonder whether God gave up on Israel. But that doesn't seem to be what the prophets think. And even more, it doesn't seem to be in character with the God we've been talking about. The God of Israel just doesn't seem like a quitter.

True enough.

On the other hand, if Jesus was always part of the plan, then why wait so long? Why go through all the heartache? Why not just start out with the new covenant we were talking about from the get-go? I mean, was it all just a game? Or did God really not know what was coming and had to improvise with Jesus?

These are great questions. Just the kind that Christians have struggled with through the ages.

It's always nice to be in good company!

You definitely are.

Part of the answer rests, I suppose, in whether you believe there was a plan in the first place.

What do you mean?

The questions you've framed all operate under the assumption that there's this divine plan God put in place, and we just watch as the various parts of it unfold.

You mean there *isn't* a plan?

Many Christians, and certainly a number of biblical authors, assume there is.

Okay then.

But there's a problem with that theory.

Yes?

What about human freedom?

What do you mean?

It's a question you raised earlier when we were talking about sin. You asked whether we are really free to sin or not sin, and it was a great question. It's worth asking again now with regard to God's plan. Do you see what I mean?

Not sure.

Think about this: If God has a divine plan that unfolds across the centuries, what does that say about us? Are we just playing various roles assigned to us? Do we have choices? Are we really free?

I hadn't really thought of that in this case. I've always found it kind of comforting to think that everything happens according to some kind of larger plan.

I think you're probably not alone in that. But what do you think now?

I think that I definitely *don't* like the idea of having no freedom, like we're all just cogs in some big machine, even if it's a divine machine. But does that mean God doesn't have a plan? That God's just reacting, making things up as God goes along?

How does that idea strike you?

To tell you the truth, not much better. As much as I value human freedom, I'd like to think there's a little more to what's going on here than one contingency plan after another or, worse, a series of random events.

I know what you mean: that's not a terribly comforting thought either.

And isn't God supposed to know everything? How do you balance that with human freedom?

Like I said, these are great questions.

Which is why I'm looking for a great answer! So what is it?

I'm not sure there is one.

What do you mean?

I mean, I don't think there is any clear or simple answer. The Bible— and here it's important to remember that the Bible is essentially a library with a number of books and authors—holds both positions and then some. Some writers believe that there is a plan and that God is in control. Some stress human freedom and responsibility. Some seem to think that there's an ultimate plan but lots of room for how it gets worked out in the meantime, while others suggest a kind of dynamic interplay between God's will and ours.

That's not very helpful.

Maybe not in terms of settling the issue once and for all, but I actually do find it kind of helpful in terms of making sense of my life in light of the Christian faith.

How so?

Well, I experience life as fairly complicated, and a lot of important things don't seem to fit into nice neat boxes. So I get a little leery when someone suggests a simple answer to really complex questions, and I appreciate that the biblical authors also found some things too difficult to reduce to simple categories. Not everything in life is black and white, and seeing different biblical authors come to different conclusions about these complex questions is kind of comforting.

I see what you mean, but wouldn't it be easier if they all just agreed?

From what you've said, it sounds like you don't always agree with your family members.

No, I don't.

What about your friends—do you agree with them all the time?

No. Of course not.

But you respect them.

Absolutely.

Do you ever find the disagreements helpful?

I suppose I do. Even the conversation we're having right now is shaped by the numerous conversations I've had with my sister and brother. We don't agree on all that much when it comes to religion, to be honest, but I'm still kind of carrying their opinions around with me as I think this through. And I bet that's true in general—that even if I don't think of it in the moment, over the long haul I probably think things through more and make better decisions because I'm around people who don't always just agree with me.

I think something similar is going on with the Bible. It's helpful to remember that the Bible, as we've said before, isn't a textbook with facts or a constitution with laws. Instead, it is a collection of confessions of faith that, together, tell the story of God and the people of God. People made these confessions at various times in history and while facing all kinds of different situations. This naturally results in a variety of opinions and points of view. And while they might not always line up neatly, they give us a depth and breadth of perspective that helps us to apply our own faith to all the different circumstances we find ourselves in.

That goes back to the idea of a family scrapbook. We might have some crazy aunts and uncles who have contributed some unusual stuff, but it's still all part of what it means to be part of this family.

Exactly.

That's helpful, but I'm still interested in this question of whether God's original plan worked or failed, or whether there was any plan to begin with. I realize that maybe we can't settle the issue, but is there *anything* we can say?

I think that when you read the Bible carefully, it's clear that God is a God of love, that God is committed to this world and the people God created, and that God intends to restore our broken relationships with God and with each other.

There's the relationship thing again.

Right. Further, I think God made all those promises—both the big covenantal promises and also the many and varied small ones—precisely because God loves and is totally committed to restoring God's creation. At the same time, I don't think we know how that's going to work out, and I think God's left a lot of room for us to participate. Not just play a role, but actually participate in the world God made. And that means this: God may very well bring things to a good end, but it's probably going to be something of a wild ride in the meantime. So, you were looking for an answer. What do you think about that one?

I think "wild ride" would certainly be a pretty good name for the biblical history of ancient Israel so far. But what about Jesus? Is he part of the original plan, or is God improvising, starting over again with a new plan?

PLAN A ᵒʳ
PLAN B?

I think I'd rather talk about God's "promise" than "plan."

Why?

I'm just not sure "plan" is all that helpful. Again, "plan" feels more like a blueprint for human history and life. Not really what I experience. Is there a plan? Maybe. Who really knows? Does God make promises? Absolutely. Does God keep those promises? The Bible confesses that God does.

So Jesus is a part of God keeping God's promises?

I think that's a much better way of putting it. And if you thought it was a wild ride before, just wait.

What do you mean?

Well, as we've seen already, there are countless ups and downs in God's relationship with Israel.

I'll say! It's a lot more like a real relationship than you'd tend to think. I was especially amazed at some of the descriptions of God. Sure, there are places where God's portrayed as angry, but there were all those other images—God as a forlorn parent, as a betrayed lover, as a protective mother. The God of the Old Testament seems much more passionate—and so much more vulnerable—than I'd imagined.

Absolutely, and that's all about to crescendo in what happens with Jesus.

How so?

> Christians confess that, in Jesus, God became human and took
> on our life and our situation in the world—sharing our hopes and
> dreams, vulnerability and limitations. This is what Christians call the
> doctrine of the Incarnation.

**And this is what you said the early Christians fought about for nearly two
centuries?**

> Yup.

**Well, I've heard the word *incarnation* before, though I've never been totally
sure what it means.**

> *Incarnation* is a big word, but knowing where it came from will help.
> In this case, it comes from two Latin words. The first part, *in*, means
> "into."

That's easy enough.

> Sure is. And the second, *carne*, means "flesh."

"Flesh" as in "human flesh"?

> Right. Flesh as in human flesh or, for that matter, animal flesh, like
> meat.

So that's where *chili con carne* comes from? Isn't that spicy stew with meat in it?

> Yup. We've actually got a whole host of words that stem from that
> same root. *Carnal*—"of the flesh." *Carnivorous*—"flesh-eating."
> *Carnage*—"slaughter of flesh." Even *carnation*, which means "flesh-
> colored."

**So *incarnation* literally means "into flesh." Like you were saying before, in
Jesus, God became a human being?**

> That's exactly right. *Incarnation* literally means "God in the flesh" or,
> a little more crassly, "God with meat on."

**God con carne? That takes a little getting used to. And like I said earlier, it's
pretty confusing. I mean, isn't saying someone is both God and human a
contradiction in terms?**

119

There's a term for this kind of contradiction also. Something that seems like a contradiction but is nevertheless true is called a *paradox*. It's something that we can't entirely understand but still believe is very important.

I've heard my sister say something like that, and I've watched my brother get really mad when she does. He thinks that Christianity is always asking us to believe things we can't understand. And she thinks that part of being Christian is taking it all on faith.

I think I can sympathize a little with each of them. Like your sister, I don't think we can understand everything. We're talking about God after all. But, like your brother, I also don't think we should just believe it because someone tells us to. I do think there are some things that are worth believing, even if I can't understand them. I believe them because something important is at stake.

What do you mean?

Some things seem to communicate a truth that's really important. And so, even though I don't understand *how* it's true, it makes a difference when I believe it *is* true. It helps me make sense not only of the rest of the biblical story but also of my life. So I accept it's true even if it goes beyond what I can understand.

And you think that's the case with the Incarnation?

Yes, I do. Maybe sharing a couple of analogies, or stories, that try to get at the deeper truth of the Incarnation will help. No story can fully explain a paradox, and each has its own limitations, but sometimes they can help fill in the larger picture of what's at stake in the doctrine.

That sounds like a good idea.

Okay, then I'll try two pretty well-known ones. The first comes from a guy named Søren Kierkegaard, a Danish philosopher who lived in the early nineteenth century. He described the Incarnation as being like a royal king who fell in love with a lowly serving girl. How could the king earn her love? He couldn't do it by a show of power, or she would be intimidated. And he couldn't just pour riches on her or decree that she was his equal. Then she might just love him for what he could give her, not for who he really is. So he became a humble servant like her in order to win her genuine love. For Kierkegaard, that helped explain the paradox of the Incarnation. It tells us *why* God became human even if we can't understand *how*.

So Kierkegaard thought that God became human in order to win our love.

Right.

But God wanted our love for the right reasons. God became human so we wouldn't love God because we were afraid or just for what God can do for us, but we'd love God for who and what God really is.

Exactly.

That helps. It gives me a reason why Christians would believe this. And the other story?

I'm not sure who wrote this one. It's about a man, a farmer who never went to church, even though his wife did regularly. Well, one cold and blustery Christmas Eve, after his wife had again pleaded with him but couldn't convince him to come with her to church, he was reading comfortably by the fire when he heard a thudding against the windows of their house. He looked out and saw that sparrows, trying to get out of the cold harsh wind and attracted by the light and heat inside, were crashing into the windows of the house. He covered the windows, but that didn't work. So he decided to put on his coat, gloves, and hat and go out and open his barn doors wide so the birds could find sanctuary there. But they wouldn't come in. He put the lights on, but they didn't come. He spread a trail of cracker crumbs, but they wouldn't follow. He tried to shoo them in, but that only frightened them more.

"If only," he thought, "I could become a sparrow for a little while, I could lead them into the barn to safety." And in that moment he realized that's what Christmas Eve—the story of God being born as a human—was all about.

So in this story God comes to us in a form we can recognize and understand, in order to communicate to us and lead us to safety.

Right. It's about the gap between humans and God that God decides to close in order to help us.

Again, very interesting.

No story is perfect, of course, but what do you think?

Well, they each help me get a sense of why the Incarnation matters. I like Kierkegaard's emphasis on love, which lines up with the God of original blessing and covenant that we've talked about. And I like the second story because God really can't sit on the sidelines and so gets involved by becoming one of the sparrows.

On the whole, I can definitely see why it took the early Christians a long time to sort all this stuff out. But you said they really fought about it, too, and I'm not sure I understand why. I mean, the Incarnation is a little confusing, sure, but controversial? What was the big deal?

The biggest issue was whether Jesus was God or human or something in between. And it didn't help that the Bible isn't crystal clear on what it says about Jesus. There are passages that seem to support all the different sides in the controversy.

For instance?

For instance, the Gospel of John begins, "In the beginning was the Word, and the Word was with God, and the Word was God. . . . And the Word became flesh and lived among us" (John 1:1, 14).

"Became flesh"—incarnation!

Right. John's Gospel is very important when it comes to the Incarnation because John so clearly says that Jesus, the Word, was with God from the beginning and actually was and is God, and also became human.

Okay, so score one for Jesus being God. What about being human? What parts of the Bible support that point of view?

In Luke's Gospel, there are stories about Jesus as a baby and as a twelve-year-old boy before the stories about him as an adult. Luke closes out a story from Jesus' childhood by saying, "And Jesus increased in wisdom and in years" (Luke 2:52).

So he grew wiser as he got older, just like we do when we grow up . . . hope-fully! That does make him sound pretty human.

So what did the Christian leaders do?

You mean after a couple of centuries of arguments, controversies, councils, and compromises?

Yeah, after that.

They ended up saying he was both, fully human *and* fully God.

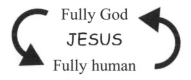

Fully God
JESUS
Fully human

Sounds like the perfect compromise—if a little hard to wrap my mind around!

There certainly was a lot of compromising, and it definitely can be challenging to understand. But not everyone thought it was perfect. In fact, there were two huge controversies about the doctrine of the Incarnation that both led up to and followed the original agreements. Each reveals something really important about the way Christians understand Jesus and the larger story of God and the world.

Okay, I'm game: What was controversy number one?

Some Christians argued that saying Jesus was God meant that Christianity was no longer monotheistic.

Hold on. Mono-what?

Sorry. Monotheistic. Again, breaking it down helps. *Mono* means "one" and *theo* means "God," so *monotheistic* literally means "believing in one God."

But what's the problem? Isn't Christianity monotheistic?

Yes, but some wondered how you could have a God in heaven who created the earth and all things, and at the same time a God on the earth—Jesus, walking and talking and eating and all the rest.

Ah, I see. That's a pretty good question when you think about it.

Yes, it was, and it started a huge controversy about whether Jesus really existed from the very beginning with God and as God, as John says, or whether Jesus was created by God—maybe first, before everything else, but still created.

You mean sort of a demi-god, like in Greek mythology or the Percy Jackson books?

Very much like that.

Frankly, this idea of Jesus being a demi-god is a little easier to understand. Given the different biblical passages you mentioned earlier, why didn't folks just go with this view?

A lot of them did. At the height of the controversy, they'd actually hold rallies, like we sometimes do today, and wave their banners and sing their songs.

Wait a minute. They had rally songs?

Sure. The most popular was really more of a chant than a song, but it was essentially, "There was a time when he was not."

Catchy. But what does it mean?

That Jesus isn't eternal. He might be divine, but he was created, and so there was a time before he was created when only God existed. "There was a time when he was not."

I'd love to hear it set to music. But seriously, this doesn't sound that unreasonable. What was the problem?

A lot of people liked it just fine. But Athanasius, a monk and leader of the church in northern Africa, felt that if Jesus is the embodiment of God's promises, then he'd better be eternal.

Why?

Because if he was created, he might also someday be un-created.

Huh?

Well, everything that is created will one day cease to exist—people, plants and animals, the earth, even the universe. So if Jesus wasn't God, but was part of God's creation, then eventually Jesus will cease to exist.

And then what would happen to the promise?

Exactly. If God is going to make you a promise—particularly a promise about raising you from the dead and redeeming the whole cosmos—you want that promise to come from God, not from a demi-god, angel, or superhuman. You want the promise from God so that you know you can trust it. In this sense, Jesus is God's "enfleshed promise."

So how did they deal with the charge that this meant Christianity now had two Gods?

Great question.

Thanks.

And a difficult one, too. The short version of the story is that the early church leaders searched the Scriptures, thought long and hard about it all, and tried out a variety of ways to explain it. They ended up saying that the Christian God revealed in the Bible is one God who simultaneously exists in three persons—the Father, the Son, and the Holy Spirit.

Well, that's about as confusing a statement as I've ever heard!

Yeah, it really is. It's called the doctrine of the Trinity, but we're not going to spend a lot of time on it here, because we're focusing on the major plotline of the Bible's story of God and the people of God.

Because the Trinity isn't a part of the story?

It is, but it's not so much a part of the plot in the sense that something actually happens—like the creation, the fall into sin, or the giving of the covenant and the law—as it is the early Christians' reflection on the plotline.

Part of the church tradition. I get it. Still, it'd be nice to understand it a little.

Well, Augustine, whom we talked about earlier, used to describe the Trinity as love. In any loving *relationship*—which is a single thing—there is someone who loves, someone who is being loved, and the love shared between the two—that's three things. Or some other early church leaders used to describe the Trinity as something like sunshine—one thing—that comes from the sun itself, sheds light, and warms us when we feel it on our face—three things. When I was a kid, my mom used to describe it to me.

Wait a sec. Your mom used to talk theology with you when you were a kid?

Well, yeah.

Was she a pastor, too?

No. She was a schoolteacher. I've been saying all along that theology is for everyone.

Yeah, I guess so, but I can't get over that you were talking about this as a kid.

Actually, you'd be surprised how many questions kids have about God.

Maybe. In any case, you were saying about your mom . . .

Yeah, my mom used to describe the Trinity as being like H_2O.

Water?

Water can be either steam, liquid, or ice—one thing that can take shape in three ways.

Very interesting, and helpful, too, actually.

I always thought so, but then I learned that something just like that was declared a heresy in the fourth century, but that's another story.

Your mom was a heretic?

To tell you the truth, good theologians always run the risk of a little heresy, but let's not tell my mom.

Deal.

So does it make a little more sense?

Yes, though the key word definitely is "little."

I get that. To be honest, I don't think anyone completely understands the Trinity, and I wouldn't trust someone if they said they did. That's why you have folks like Augustine offering analogies. They're not perfect, but they help to give you an idea of what's at stake.

And the key thing at stake in the Trinity is that Jesus, the Son, really is God, so that we could trust the—what did you call it—the "enfleshed promise" that God makes in him?

Exactly.

And this is what they fought about?

Fiercely. Even though Athanasius was a bishop over much of what is today Egypt and Libya, he was exiled five different times during his life.

Exiled? You mean he was . . .

Kicked out of his own country. That's right. Which might help explain some of the severe language he uses when defending his position and attacking his opponents.

So, curious minds want to know: What did he say?

His major opponents followed a guy named Arius, one of the major supporters of the "there was a time when he was not" platform. And so he would write against the people he described as "Ariomaniacs."

I like it. I can just see Athanasius riding his donkey out of town for the fifth time, scribbling away, "Cursed by the Ariomaniacs . . . ."

That picture's probably not too far from what happened.

But he eventually won?

Yeah, though not completely until a long time after his death. Eventually, though, the church agreed with Athanasius that God's promises had better come straight from God.

And Christians still believe this all these centuries later.

Well, Christians today, as back then, disagree about plenty of things, including the Incarnation, but most Christians still believe that Jesus was really God, and so we can trust the promises he made to us.

So the Incarnation is first and foremost about God making a promise.

That's right. A promise made in the flesh and blood of Jesus, a promise about new and abundant life, a promise that God is fundamentally on our side, a promise that death doesn't have the last word. And all these promises are promises we can trust because God made them, and God will keep them.

Very cool.
Okay, so what was the second big controversy?

Interestingly, the second argument came from the other side.

The other side?

Well, if Arius had a hard time with the idea that Jesus was really God, a guy named Marcion, and a number of others, had a hard time saying that Jesus was really human.

Really? How come?

Because they had a very clear and very strong sense that God was perfect, that God was immortal, that God was entirely good.

And are they wrong?

No. But they contrasted this very good and very perfect God with fallen, sinful creation, and they couldn't imagine God getting too involved in this messed-up world. And they certainly couldn't fathom God becoming a part of the mess through the Incarnation. They thought it was all a little beneath God.

So what did they make of Jesus?

They thought Jesus was thoroughly divine and only appeared to be human because there was no way the holy God of the universe could become human.

Where did they get that idea?

Actually, the Bible. For instance, we have John describing Jesus as the eternal Word of God. And then in Luke's Gospel, Jesus says just before dying, "Father, into your hands I commend my spirit" (23:46). They took that verse as a sign that Jesus' divine spirit had used a human body kind of like a disguise, but had never really become human.

Boy, the Bible really does say a lot of different things. No wonder they were confused.

Absolutely.

So at heart they believed that they were defending the idea of God's perfect goodness?

Exactly.

Again, that makes some sense. So what was at stake this time? Why didn't the early Christians side with Marcion?

To get at this, it might help to share part of a letter that Tertullian, another early church leader, wrote to Marcion.

A letter? Were they friends?

Far from it. Actually, it's written as an address to Marcion and people who agreed with him. But it's actually a paper against Marcion and his ideas. In fact, its title is simply "Against Marcion."

He didn't beat around the bush, did he?

Not at all.

So what did he have to say to Marcion?

First, it's useful to know that Tertullian himself was a very strict monk, an ascetic, actually.

A what?

An "ascetic" is someone who believes that to be really spiritual you need to avoid the worldly pleasures of life. The word comes from a

Greek word for "training," like an athlete in training, and so they try to train their bodies to escape, as much as possible, the physical, carnal life of the body in order to attain spiritual goals.

That sounds a lot like Marcion.

Marcion teaching from his version of Scripture

Quintus Florens Tertullian, 160–220, church father and theologian

Exactly, which is what makes Tertullian's argument with Marcion all the more interesting. You'd think he'd agree that the Incarnation—precisely because it's about God becoming, well, carnal—is a little hard to handle, if not outright scandalous. So here's what he writes:

> Come, then, start with the birth itself, the object of aversion, and run through your catalogue: the filth of the generative seeds within the womb, of the bodily fluid and blood; the loathsome, curdled lump of flesh which has to be fed for nine months off this same muck. Describe the womb—expanding daily, heavy, troubled, uneasy even in sleep, torn between the impulses of fastidious distaste and those of excessive hunger. . . .

Not exactly the kind of guy you'd want in the delivery room!

Just wait. It gets even better:

> Undoubtedly you are also horrified at the infant, the infant which has been brought into the world together with its after birth.

Sheesh, he spares no details.

What's weird, though, is that as I listen to Tertullian go after Marcion, I actually find myself more and more sympathetic with Marcion. I mean, child-birth is a miracle, but it's also really, really messy. We tend to think about Jesus as a cute little baby in the manger, which is sweet. But when you put it that way—describing the way it actually was—it does seem a little beneath God's dignity to get wrapped up in the messy, mucky world of human biology.

No kidding. I remember thinking the same thing when my son, our first child, was born.

Hold on. Your wife is delivering a baby and you're thinking about the Incarnation?!

Well, I guess I couldn't help it. I mean, I was there helping as much as I could, but I also couldn't help but think about how incredible, really pretty unbelievable, it is that we confess that God was born like this—such a mess, so vulnerable, so totally earthy.

So what did Tertullian have to say about all that?

Actually, it's right here that Tertullian is at his best: "You repudiate such veneration of nature, do you . . . ?" he writes (and at this point I imagine him kind of rearing up to point a long, bony finger at Marcion), "But how were *you* born?"*

Oh my goodness! I get it! If human birth is too messy for God, then so are we. But by becoming human—even by being born as we are—God in Jesus totally promises that God is for us, that God is on our side.

That's exactly right. In the Incarnation God not only assures us that God can understand all of our ups and downs, dreams and disappointments, hopes and fears, but also that God will never give up on us. John Calvin, a Swiss theologian from the sixteenth century, used to describe it as "God's condescension"—God giving up heaven and glory to take on our life.

---

*From Tertullian's *Adversus Marcionem* (chapter IV), which can be found in various free online translations.

It's like God in Jesus grabs hold of us—all of us—and won't let go.

That's the promise the Incarnation makes.

Which means that God is with my dad in his illness, and God understands the anger and pain my friend feels.

That's part of why I think the Incarnation is really important.

I agree. It doesn't answer everything, but it helps me to not feel so alone. Sometimes when my sister talks about God, it just seems like God could heal my dad at any time but isn't healing him because, I don't know, we aren't praying enough, or Dad doesn't have enough faith, or it's all part of some big plan.

(That's when my brother gets really mad, by the way.)

But this is a different picture of God. It's a picture of God being with us, holding on to us. I'd still like to know what God's going to do about it all, but it helps a lot to know that God isn't just sitting up in heaven watching. God is really with us.

I agree. And that's actually what one of the names Jesus has been called means. *Emmanuel* is Hebrew for "God is with us."

As in "O Come, O Come, Emmanuel."

Right. We sing and pray that God would come and really be with us.
In Jesus, that is exactly what God did.

So no wonder Tertullian stressed Jesus' humanity. It's the only way we can know God won't ultimately desert us.

Exactly. At the heart of the doctrine of the Incarnation is the promise that God loves us just the way we are.

Say more—this suddenly sounds pretty important.

You're right; it is important. The early Christians believed that part of what is at the heart of the Incarnation is an affirmation of the original blessing that is part of creation. Despite sin, God still believes we're worthy of loving, of holding on to, of redeeming. Why else come to us in our own flesh? And so even if it's confusing to say that God in Jesus is both human and divine, both parts are just too important to give up.

Jesus is divine so that we can trust God's enfleshed promises. That was Athanasius's point. And Jesus is human so that we know God is really coming for us, people who are also of the flesh. That was Tertullian's point.

Right. And while Tertullian had already made the point, it took a little while to sink in how important it was to keep stressing that Jesus really did take on our life, our flesh, our condition. Martin Luther, who lived more than a thousand years after Tertullian, used to say that you can't press Jesus too deeply into the flesh.

What did he mean?

Just that it's so much easier for us to imagine that God is spirit, hovering somewhere out there, in the distance, watching and waiting.

But the God of Scripture doesn't sit on the sidelines.

Right again. This God gets involved.

Okay, so I get how important it is to hold these two things—divine and human—together, even if it's hard. But I also have to say that you're right; it's so much easier to imagine God as spirit than as flesh.

Except that then you can never be really sure that God loves you, just as you are. Not the person you want to become, not the person you promised to become, not the person you're trying to become or pretending to already be, but you, just as you are—in the flesh, fallen, sinful, insecure, regularly missing the mark. That means that there's nothing in you that's so awful as to make you unlovable. That there's nothing that you can do, or that can happen to you, that will keep God from loving you. It's a huge promise.

I think I get it. The Incarnation is God's promise that God loves us. No matter where we go, God will come after us. No matter what happens to us, God will hold on to us. No matter what happens in this life, God will not let us go.

No matter what. The apostle Paul said that nothing—not even life and death—can separate us from the love of God (Romans 8:37-39).

I like that. And that's what the Incarnation is finally about?

It's a big part of it. By becoming one of us in Jesus, God is telling us that we are still inherently, intrinsically worthy and deserving of God's love. Sin, whatever problems it has caused our relationships with God and each other, has not changed that.

I think it also means that God understand us, including our hopes and fears, our joys and anger. I was with my friend once when she was really mad—at the guy who hit her with his car, at herself for taking so long to recover, and at God for not doing something to prevent it. Later, I asked if she ever felt guilty about getting so mad. She said she felt guilty when she got mad at people, but not at God. God, she said, would understand.

I think that's right. There's a verse in the Letter to the Hebrews, which is a book in the New Testament, that says, "For we do not have a high priest"—meaning Jesus—"who is unable to sympathize with our weaknesses, but we have one who in every respect has been tested as we are, yet without sin" (Hebrews 4:15).

Exactly. I think that's important, too.

You're right. All of these things—that God loves us, that God promises not to abandon us, that God understands what it's like to be us—all of these are part of what the Incarnation is trying to tell us.

So why does God do it? I mean, it sounds really risky. Becoming human, anything could have happened.

And a lot did happen. But I think that just brings us back to the question of why God creates and gives us creation in the first place. It's just in God's nature to create out of love, to share that creation with us out of love, and to take a risk on us, also out of love. And because this is all a part of who God just *is*, then I think God can't help reaching out to us, any more than I could help reaching out to my daughter or son if one of them were in trouble.

That is a powerful promise, and I'm glad we've talked about it all. It's comforting to know that when it comes to the struggles my dad and friend and lots of other people are having, God's not just sitting around impassively or waiting for them to have enough faith. Instead, God is really present with them and for them.

I'm really glad it's been helpful.

Yes, it definitely has. And to be honest, it feels even bigger than just the problems my dad and friend have been having. Because trusting that God cares, really cares and understands, makes it more possible to believe in God at all. I don't think this is necessarily the picture of God that my siblings and I grew up with, and it's definitely not the picture that a lot of the anti-religious books write about. I wonder if even my brother might consider a God like this.

Like we said near the beginning of our conversation, *how* you imagine God to be—whether stern, loving, vengeful, caring, or something else—makes all the difference.

Yeah, it really does, and so this has been very helpful. At the same time, though . . .

Yes?

Well, there are two things that keep nagging at me. First, I guess I'd still like to see God get a little more active. I mean, I appreciate that God is with us in our suffering, but can we expect anything more?

That's a great question. Let's not forget that God also is at work through us, and through the doctors and nurses and others who are caring for your dad, your friend, and others who are sick, just as God is at work through all kinds of people and agencies to help anyone who is suffering.

True, and it's helpful to remember that God continues to care and create through us.

But I still know what you mean. It's one thing to empathize with us; it's another to actually do something, to save us.

That's it exactly!

And in the incarnation of Jesus—and in his life and ministry—God is at work to redeem the world, actively and purposefully, and that's something we will talk about. But before going there, you said you had another question, too.

Well, I've been thinking back to the two stories that you told to help give a picture of what's at stake in the Incarnation. And they're helpful and all, but from what I know of the story of Jesus, it doesn't seem to end quite as nicely as either of those stories. I mean, in the biblical story, Jesus ends up dead. The king who becomes a peasant in Kierkegaard's story and the farmer who becomes a sparrow don't get killed. If these stories were really analogies of the biblical story, then the serving girl would murder her new husband and the sparrows wouldn't just refuse to follow the farmer into the barn—they'd kill him. So what gives?

You're right. The biblical story is a lot darker than either of these short stories. And at this point I think both of the questions you just raised are connected.

How so?

Because when God becomes human, God isn't only making us a promise or telling us God loves us or even showing us the way. God is, in fact, doing all that, but also more. When God becomes human, God is entering into a world of sin with the intention of winning back lost humanity, with the desire to restore a fallen creation. And given how deeply creation—and all of us—are enmeshed in sin, that's going to be quite a struggle. Or, to put it another way, when God becomes human in order to win us back from sin and death, that spells trouble.

Sounds like that's what we should turn to next.

God is both divine + human

Insights and Questions

Incarnation is a promise that
God loves us the way we
are. He is with us in our
suffering. He will not let
us go. He will hold onto
us. No matter what happens
to us.

CHAPTER 6

Life Wins

Atonement

I feel a little bit like we've been watching a two-part cliffhanger and we just finished the first part. You know, where the last words on the screen are "To be continued. . . ."

What do you mean?

Well, we spent a lot of time trying to understand the Incarnation. Not so much *how* it could happen, but *why*. And there was a lot to talk about, because the Incarnation shows us that God loves us, won't give up on us, and understands us. But then everything turned a little darker, actually a lot darker.

Say more about that.

Well, suddenly it seemed that there was another reason God became human—to rescue or save us from sin. And I liked that because I want to see God get a little more active. But I'm not yet sure what that means. And it sounds like that last part—wanting to fix what's wrong—is exactly what got Jesus killed.

I think you're right on both counts. Yes, God comes to us in Jesus to show us how much God loves us. But you're also right that God comes to deal with the problem of sin we've talked about.

Because covenant, law, and community were helpful, but in the end they didn't do the trick. I mean, they may have helped us *cope* with our fallen condition, but they don't *change* it. Is that right?

That's certainly the testimony of the prophets—that covenant and law continue to be God's good gift to us, to help us treat each other as God desires. But in the end we're still stuck in sin, still unable to trust as we should, and so we still do great damage to ourselves and each other. So God needs to do something more dramatic; God needs to create something new.

Which is the other reason Jesus comes.

Right. Jesus comes to announce the coming of God's kingdom.

"Kingdom." That's not a word we use very much in a democracy. What does he mean by that?

What comes to mind when you hear the word?

Kings, naturally, and castles and soldiers to protect the realm, I guess.

That's not so different than what people thought during Jesus' day. When you talked about a kingdom, it would be natural to think about the Roman Empire and Caesar, if you were a Roman. Or if you were Jewish, you might think about King David and the restoration of Israel.

What do you mean by "restoration"?

Under King David and some of his descendants, Israel enjoyed a time of relative peace and prosperity. But for much of its history, Israel was either divided or conquered or both. By the time Jesus came, Israel was ruled by the Romans, and the people wanted desperately to be liberated from Roman rule and have their own government restored.

So that's a pretty interesting environment for Jesus to talk about the kingdom of God!

Exactly. It actually caused a fair amount of confusion, because the kingdom Jesus was announcing wasn't a military kingdom like either Caesar's or David's, but it was instead a whole new way of being in relationship with each other and with God.

I can totally understand why people would hear Jesus talk about a kingdom and get excited about the possibility of throwing out the Romans. But if that's *not* what Jesus was talking about, what did he mean? What's different about God's kingdom?

If we think back to the story of creation, it doesn't really seem like the idea at the beginning was to have some people rule over others. Instead, it seems like Adam and Eve were intended to live in partnership with each other. Setting up another king, even a good king, would still keep in place the essential pecking order we use to deal with our original insecurity.

I hadn't thought about that.

Interestingly, it's not God who wants a king in the first place. It's the Israelites who ask for a king so that they can be like the other nations and because they think a king will give them better protection. God does allow that move, but warns that it will introduce even greater inequality among people (1 Samuel 8).

And so Jesus is calling for a kingdom without kings, a kingdom of equals? The first democracy?

I don't know if I'd go quite that far. I think that Jesus is less interested in setting up a government and more interested in restoring our relationship with God. In turn, that would help us heal and restore our relationships with each other and with all creation.

It might be interesting to look briefly at a story from the very beginning of Jesus' ministry when he goes into the wilderness and is tempted:

> *Then Jesus was led up by the Spirit into the wilderness to be tempted by the devil. He fasted forty days and forty nights, and afterwards he was famished. The tempter came and said to him, "If you are the Son of God,*

command that these stones become loaves of bread." But he answered, "It is written, 'One does not live by bread alone, but by every word that comes from the mouth of God.'" Then the devil took him to the holy city and places him on the pinnacle of the temple, saying to him, "If you are the Son of God, throw yourself down; for it is written, 'He will command his angels concerning you,' and 'On their hands they will bear you up, so that you will not dash your foot against a stone.'" Jesus said to him, "Again it is written, 'Do not put the LORD your God to the test.'" Again, the devil took him to a very high mountain and showed him all the kingdoms of the world and their splendor; and he said to him, "All these I will give you, if you will fall down and worship me." Jesus said to him, "Away with you, Satan! For it is written, 'Worship the LORD your God, and serve only him.'" Then the devil left him, and suddenly angels came and waited on him. (Matthew 4:1-11)

Wow. I can't get over how much this scene reminds me of when Adam and Eve are tempted.

How so?

Well, the devil comes and creates insecurity, mistrust: "*If* you are the Son of God . . ." The "if" makes it seem like maybe it's not true. Then the devil invites, or really tempts, Jesus to prove his identity for himself. If he just turns stones into bread or throws himself off the temple and is saved, he'll know for sure he's God's Son. And if he worships the devil, then he'll receive everything he could possibly want.

And how does Jesus deal with, as we called it before, his own "God-shaped hole" and the temptation to fill it with all the stuff the devil offers?

Weird, I never thought of Jesus having a hole like we do.

That's what the verse from Hebrews means, I think. That he was just like us, tested in every way (Hebrews 4:15). So how does Jesus deal with it?

He quotes the Bible. Which I guess means that, unlike Adam and Eve, he trusts God.

Right. And, again unlike Adam and Eve, he deals with his original insecurity by defining himself through his relationship with God, not by trying to be independent, trying to be like God, or finding something else to worship instead of God.

Interesting. By remaining dependent on God he actually is free to be who God created him to be.

But how does that relate to the kingdom?

Because that's the kind of kingdom Jesus is bringing, a kingdom where we all live in mutual dependence on God and each other. In this way we are free to be who we were created to be. We don't have to prove ourselves. We don't have to define ourselves against each other. We don't have to use people we were meant to love and try to fill our hole with things we were meant to use. And so after this temptation, Jesus goes out teaching and preaching and healing and feeding and welcoming all kinds of people, and by doing all this he models the kind of kingdom God will bring.

I can understand how that kind of kingdom is, in a sense, the opposite of the sinful human condition we talked about—the kind of kingdom where we *don't* define ourselves *against* each other but instead through our relationships *with* each other and God. But I can't understand why anyone would kill him for that.

Well, think about it. If you're invested in the way things are, if you've acquired a certain amount of power or occupy a place near the top of the pecking order, then the kind of kingdom Jesus brings isn't very attractive. And even if you're lower down on the pecking order, there's still a certain security in knowing your place. And so in parable after parable, and in miracle after miracle, Jesus announced that God looks at things differently. It's not about pecking orders. God's kingdom of restored relationships is breaking into—and therefore upsetting—the kingdoms of the world.

Can you give an example?

How much time do you have?

But seriously, there are tons of examples. Maybe we should start with one of his most famous parables, the Prodigal Son.

Sure, I recognize that one. It's about the son who runs away and blows his inheritance, and then when he comes crawling back home, his father welcomes him back.

> That's right. It's interesting, though, to pay attention to why Jesus tells the parable in the first place. Luke sets it up this way: "Now all the tax collectors and sinners were coming near to listen to him. And the Pharisees and the scribes were grumbling and saying, 'This fellow welcomes sinners and eats with them.' So he told them this parable" (Luke 15:1-3).

I gather the Pharisees and scribes are the people with the power; at least they sound like they're considered better than the "sinners" Luke mentions.

> Right. The Pharisees are very devoted religious leaders, kind of like the elders or church council members of today's congregation. And scribes were experts in the Old Testament law. On the other side of the spectrum are, as you noticed, sinners, which could refer to all manner of folks but definitely describes people who everyone knew were living sinful lives. And tax collectors were included because they worked with the occupying Roman forces to collect taxes and so were universally despised.

And these are the people who are coming to Jesus?

> Think about it. Who's going to appreciate Jesus' message about everyone being welcomed, about everyone being forgiven, more than the people who know they are down and out? And so, when the Pharisees and scribes grumble about the company he's keeping, Jesus tells them three parables, each one about something or someone that is lost. The Prodigal Son is the last and longest of those parables and reinforces the idea that Jesus has come especially for those who are lost, alone, and rejected, the down and out.

Even though they might have brought this on themselves? I mean, what if they chose to be a tax collector or to lead a sinful life? Shouldn't they be held accountable?

But which of us isn't caught up in some kind of sin and in the larger sinful condition of humanity more generally? Maybe the sins you and I commit don't seem as big, or as public, but I think it's safe to say that we're also caught up in the general tendency of humans to not trust God but to look out for ourselves. So I think that part of Jesus' message is that when we set up pecking orders for who's in and who's out, and maybe especially when it comes to morality, we miss that we're no better than the tax collectors and sinners.

So it almost sounds like there's just no difference in God's eyes. That no one, when it comes to standing before God, is worse than anyone else. And no one deserves more than anyone else; we've all missed the mark.

That's right. There may be greater consequences from some sins than others—that is, more harm may be done. But when it comes to our basic relationship with God, we all are in the same boat. Jesus gets at this pretty directly in another parable about a businessman who needs some temporary workers. He goes out and hires some first thing in the morning. But later in the day he needs more help and so hires some more workers. This happens a couple of times until he hires the last group about an hour before quitting time. When it comes time to pay the workers at the end of the day, he pays the guys who worked just an hour first and gives them a whole day's wages. When the guys who worked all day come, they also get a whole day's wages, and they're really mad (Matthew 20:1-16).

No kidding. I would be, too, if I'd worked so much longer than the other guys.

Right, but as Jesus points out, the businessman did exactly what he promised to do—pay them a day's wage for a day's work—so shouldn't he be allowed to be generous with the others if he wants to?

I guess so, but it doesn't really seem fair.

But that's just it. It's not about fairness. If it was about fairness, then Adam and Eve would have died, and God would have abandoned ancient Israel, and God would hold us accountable for all of our sins, too. Finally, Jesus is establishing a kingdom that's not about who deserves what, but instead is about how much God loves *all* people.

Okay, I'm beginning to get the picture, and I can see why this would make the people in power mad. They want Jesus to play by the rules, rules they set up and benefit from. But here's where I'm a little confused. I mean, we talk about God working through Jesus' cross, but here it sounds like he was just some kind of activist or idealist who ticked off the wrong people.

Christians definitely believe God was working through the cross.

But if he preaches about God's coming kingdom of love and forgiveness, and that gets him killed, how can any of that free us from sin or restore us to right relationship with God?

That's a great—and huge—question. Christians through the centuries have offered a number of different answers to it, three main ones in particular.

Well, given that we're following the biblical plotline, which one most lines up with what the Bible says?

Actually, each of them has support in the Bible.

I was worried you'd say that.

As we've seen many times, the Bible contains a variety of voices and perspectives, each trying to make sense of their experience of God. So when it comes to something huge, like the cross, it's little wonder that there are a variety of interpretations.

I suppose that makes sense. But is one of them at least obviously better than the other two?

Well, I'm tempted to say that all of them are on the right track . . .

I'm not sure I'll be satisfied with that.

. . . and that none of them are.

Oh, come on. Now you're going too far.

Maybe. Let me explain a little.

I think that would be a good idea.

Okay, so as I said, there are three main theories about what God is up to in Jesus' death and resurrection.

Hmm. I'd almost forgotten that.

What?

Well, I keep asking why Jesus died. But it's not just his death that the Bible tells about; it's also his resurrection.

That's very true, and very important.

Okay, so you were saying—three theories.

Yes, and each one not only draws from particular parts of Scripture but also has certain things going for it.

That still sounds like you think each also comes up short.

I do. In part I think they fall short because they try to fit the cross and resurrection into a larger plan.

Like we were doing earlier with Jesus and the Incarnation, when we discussed whether he was part of the original plan or something new.

Right.

And you said you didn't find talking about a "plan" as helpful as talking about a "promise." In Jesus, God was keeping God's promises.

Exactly right. And I think these theories about the cross—they are sometimes called theories of atonement—make the same mistake.

Hold on a second. I want to hear where the theories go wrong, but first I'm interested in the word you used—*atonement*.

Yes?

Well, I typically think of atonement as making payment, or fixing things, or somehow setting things right. Isn't that what it means to atone for something?

Yes, that's often the way we use the word.

So is that what's going on in the cross? God, or Jesus, is making payment, is fixing something that's broken, making something wrong right again?

I think that's going to be one of the main things we focus on. But to get at that larger question, it might help first to look at the word *atonement* itself a little more carefully.

It sure helped with *incarnation*.

I think it will help here, too. And in a sense, it's even easier, because we don't need to know any Latin this time. *Atonement* is about the only word that the English language contributed to theology.

Really?

Take a look at the parts of the word. What do you see?

I see "at-one-ment."

Exactly.

You mean it's that simple? Atonement means making something "one" again? Like taking something that is broken, or separated, or torn apart, and bringing it together again?

That's right. Atonement is taking something that has been broken apart and mending it, putting it back together so that it is one again.

So the cross is about making whole something that's been broken?

Exactly.

And I'm betting that what was broken apart was our relationship with God.

I'd take that bet.

So how does Jesus' death . . .

. . . and resurrection . . .

Right, and resurrection. How does Jesus' death and resurrection fix or restore our broken relationship with God?

Now that's where things get really interesting. Because it really depends on what you think the primary problem is. Right? I mean, if you're going to repair something, you first need to have a sense of what was actually broken.

So we're back to sin and the human condition.

Right. And in particular, the question of how sin disrupts our relationship with God. Is sin an offense against God's honor? Is it a crime, as in breaking God's laws, that needs to be punished? Is sin a basic ignorance or immaturity? Is it a fundamental inability on our part to love God and neighbor? Christians through the centuries have suggested all these possibilities and more, and how you size up the problem greatly influences how you think atonement happens.

That makes sense.

Each theory of atonement, actually, will have something to say about us and our human predicament, about what God is primarily like, and about how to restore the relationship between God and us.

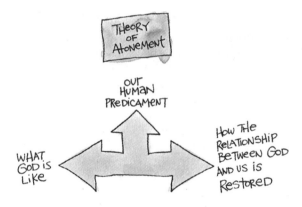

Can you say that again?

Sure. One question is "What is sin?" That is, what is our human condition and predicament? How you answer that question is tied to the question of God's fundamental character. Is God, for instance, more like a loving parent, a cosmic disciplinarian, a just king, or some combination of these? If sin is primarily a crime, about breaking God's laws, then God is concerned particularly with justice. Once you've described our situation and God's character, that makes it possible to talk about how our relationship is restored.

Three things—our problem, God's character, and how things get repaired. Okay, got it. But earlier you were saying that whatever their strengths, the three theories of atonement get off base when they make the cross part of a larger plan.

Don't get me wrong; it's not that I don't like plans in general. I think making plans is a great strategy to get work done. I just don't think everything fits into a plan. And sometimes you can miss the distinct character of an actual event, miss its real genius or effect, if you're always trying to fit it into a plan. Promises, on the other hand, are always concrete and specific, and they work only if they actually affect you.

I'm not sure I'm with you. Could you say a little more about that?

Sure. Let's start with the problem with plans. Think about how many different people you meet over the course of your life.

Okay.

Sometimes, before you get to know someone, you've heard something about the person ahead of time. It could be flattering or unflattering; either way, it shapes your expectations of what this person will be like. Or maybe you've noticed something about him or her and begin to see a pattern. That sets up your expectations, too. Now, sometimes what you've heard is right, or you've read the situation correctly. But other times, what you heard isn't accurate, or you've misread what you've seen. When that happens . . .

. . . When that happens, it's hard to really get to know the person, because you've already pretty much made up your mind about what he or she is like.

Right. Your expectations—your sense of the person—might change, but it takes longer because at first you don't interpret your expectations in light of your actual experience of the person. You interpret your experience in light of your expectations. And then you don't just miss out on the person in general but also miss out on the very specific ways that person might affect you, on the distinct relationship you might have.

Exactly. And you think this is what happens with the theories of atonement?

Yes. I think that people may organize a lot of the various "data" about the cross and resurrection in helpful ways, but they ultimately tend not only to miss some important details but also to mute the actual effect of the cross and resurrection.

Mute the cross and resurrection? I'm not sure I know what you mean.

Well, I think that by viewing the cross and resurrection as part of a larger plan, the distinct events of Jesus' cross and resurrection lose something of their character. And in this way they lose their power to affect us. It's not the cross or resurrection—let alone their effect on us—that we're paying attention to anymore. It's the specific plan that matters.

Interesting. The plan ends up being something of a box that you put the cross and resurrection into.

Well put.

And if they're in a box, then you wonder whether "at-one-ment" really happens?

Exactly. Which brings up the matter of promises.

Yeah, I was wondering about that. You said promises are always distinct and that they only work if you feel their specific effect.

That's right. Think about it. You never make a promise to someone in general. It's always very specific. That is, it's never just "I promise," it's always "I promise to come home on time," or "I promise to read to you tonight," or "I promise to kick the soccer ball around when I get home from work," or "I promise to love you and be faithful to you."

I get it. A generic promise wouldn't mean anything.

Right. And what's more, promises only work if they affect the person they're said to.

Say a little more.

We talked about this in regard to covenant, how a promise is always about the future. The promise has the power to orient the person who hears it to the future it imagines, the future it promises.

I remember. God made a covenant with Abraham and his descendants in part to draw them all into a community created by a shared expectation about the future.

And that's true of all promises. Unless a promise captures the imagination of the person it's spoken to, unless it creates a sense of that future, it doesn't work.

Which means that unless the person trusts the future it describes—really trusts the promise being made and the one making the promise—the promise has had no effect; in a sense it's failed.

That's right. You might keep your end of the promise, but if the person wasn't affected by it, it didn't work the way you'd hoped.

Which means that promises are highly relational. They're about trust.

Exactly. And whatever else we know about relationships, we know that if it's a real relationship, if the relationship is at all alive, it will affect us.

I'll say. And that's not only true of the relationships we have with each other, it's also true about the relationship we have with God. We saw that all over the place in the Bible.

Right again.

So if the theories of the atonement not only miss some of the distinctive details of the cross and resurrection but also mute their effect on us, should we just skip over the three theories and talk about a better way of understanding and experiencing the atonement that Jesus' cross and resurrection bring about?

That's tempting, especially because I know we don't have the time to go into the theories in any significant detail. They're fairly complex and very interesting.

But you've got to give the short version at least.

Sure. I think it might actually help to talk briefly about them because each of them—and the larger plan they represent—have some very definite things to say about our fundamental problem and God's fundamental character. And I think we'll be able to appreciate and experience more fully our own sense of atonement if we view it against the backdrop of the other three first.

Okay, I'm game. Which one first?

I think we should take the most popular one first.

Sounds good.

It was formulated back in the eleventh century by a theologian by the name of Anselm.

Anselm, Augustine, Athanasius, Arius—did your name have to start with an *A* to be a theologian in the old days?

You're forgetting Tertullian, not to mention Calvin, Wesley, and Luther.

True enough.

Of course there's also Thomas Aquinas, so there does seem to be a preponderance of *A* names. In any event . . .

Right, sorry.

No problem. In any event, Anselm lived in the feudal, medieval world of kings and queens, lords and peasants, and his theory is very much shaped by that world. As we already mentioned, we're particularly interested in three things each of these theories describes: our human condition and problem, God's primary character, and how God, because of God's character, solves the problem and restores our relationship.

Okay, so what does Anselm say about these three?

Well, he makes sense of them in light of the world he lives in, and the world he lives in is dominated by a sense of the king's honor and justice.

Say a little more.

In the feudal world and, indeed, for much of history, monarchy—where one person holds political power—is the primary form of government. It doesn't matter whether a king, or queen for that matter, was given the rule or took it. The fundamental assumption is that one person rules. So the only thing that keeps this kind of system from dissolving into absolute chaos and tyranny is a sense of justice.

But because it's the *king's* justice, can't the king say what justice is?

That has certainly happened. But as long as there have been kings and queens, there's also been discussion of what makes *good* kings and queens; that is, what keeps a king or queen from becoming a tyrant or despot. Plato, one of the earliest Greek philosophers, talks about it, and so does just about everyone else right up through the Middle Ages. So justice, in Anselm's world, isn't just something the king doles out; it's also something the king lives under.

How does this play out in terms of his theory of atonement?

In Anselm's scenario, God is the king.

That doesn't surprise me.

And humans are the subjects, the peasants.

Makes sense, too.

The problem arises when humans sin, hurting others, themselves, and the creation. Because from Anselm's point of view, when this happens we haven't just made a mistake—we peasants have violated the king's justice, offended the king's honor, and so we deserve death.

Kind of harsh.

Maybe, except that the survival of human society itself hangs on it. Think back to Hobbes.

The stuffed tiger, as in Calvin and Hobbes?

The other Hobbes. The seventeenth-century British philosopher who influenced the writing of the U.S. Constitution.

Oh yeah, the pessimist: life is "nasty, brutish, and short."

Or a realist, depending on your point of view. But either way, he still has a point. Which is why monarchy is crucial, and why the king's justice can't be defied. One unpunished sin, or so the theory goes, and the whole ordered system is threatened.

So humans have to be punished for their sin.

Right. Except in this case the king loves the subjects and doesn't want to punish them.

But at the same time the king has to preserve a sense of justice in order to hold up the system. Kind of like Arthur.

Sorry, you lost me.

King Arthur. He loves Guinevere, his wife, and Lancelot, his best friend and finest knight. But when they betray him by having an affair, he has to punish them. As a husband and friend, he would gladly forgive them, but as the king, he has no choice but to punish them, or there's no reason anyone should keep the law.

Exactly God's dilemma, as Anselm sees it.

And this all explains the cross?

Both the Incarnation and the cross are part of Anselm's explanation for how God achieves atonement. In fact, his major book is called *Cur Deus Homo*.

Let me guess, Latin?

Latin for "Why the God-Man?"

The God-man. That sounds like the Incarnation again. Interesting. And Anselm's answer to his own question?

Totally comes from his analysis of the problem.

Let me give it a try: God is a just and loving king with peasants—us—who have violated the king's justice and deserve death. Because God is loving, God doesn't want to punish us. But because God is just, God must punish us if justice is going to mean anything.

Okay, that part makes sense, but I'm still not sure why Jesus, the God-man, solves this.

I'll give you a hint. Anselm's theory is commonly known as the "substitutionary theory of atonement."

Substitutionary? But who's subbing for whom? Oh, wait, I get it: Jesus substitutes for us, taking our place. Then, according to Anselm, the cross is the punishment we should receive?

Right.

But how does that restore our relationship with God?

This is where the Incarnation comes in. Because Jesus is fully human, he can take our place—a human for a human. Because he's innocent, the one human being who hasn't sinned, he doesn't deserve punishment, so he's clearly being punished not for his sins but for ours. And because he's God, his sacrifice counts for all of us. It's not just a life for a life, but the life of the God-man for all of humanity.

Hmm. So that's why there's a God-man.

What do you think?

Well, there's no denying there's a certain logic to it all. Legally, it makes great sense. If justice is going to prevail—and justice has to prevail—then someone has to suffer for the sins of humanity.

That pretty much sums it up.

So in terms of our three concerns: Our human problem is that we've offended God's honor and broken God's law and justice.

God's primary characteristic is justice. I mean, God loves us, but God's kingly justice needs to be satisfied before God can express that love to us.

Once the demands of justice are satisfied, then we are restored to relationship with God.

Right on the money.
So what do you think?

I can definitely see why this would have appeal. It's almost like a divine accounting balance sheet. On the debit side is all of our sin, a debt so huge we can never pay it. On the credit side is Jesus, totally innocent and the Son of God to boot. So an inconceivably huge debt is canceled, paid back, by Jesus' death on the cross.

But . . .

But?

But if it's logical, it seems like a cold, calculating logic.

What do you mean?

Well, it's the logic of the legal courts, or of the accounting firms, but I'm not sure it's the logic of real life, and definitely not the logic of relationships. I mean, justice prevails, sure, but what happens to mercy? Can you imagine if we ran our lives this way? We talked about this earlier—keeping count of every slight or injury done to us by friend, family member, or coworker, refusing to be in relationship until they'd paid us back or were punished? It would be a nightmare. Like I said, I actually know some people who are always counting, keeping track of all the bad things that happen to them and the good things that happen to others. Believe me, they're miserable.

I gather Anselm's theory isn't for you, then.

I don't think it's just a matter of personal taste. I actually think it doesn't much reflect the God we've been talking about all this time. I see original sin, but where's original blessing? I see law and the threat of punishment, but where's covenant and community? I see the cold logic of a judge and king, but where's the passionate embrace of a parent desperate to be in relationship with a wayward child?

You're on a roll.

And I'm not done. Life isn't all about justice, thank goodness; it's also about mercy, forgiveness, and love. You realize as you grow up that some scores just can't be settled. So I've forgiven others because I love them, and others have forgiven me. Even when that's difficult, it's always amazing. Why couldn't God do the same? I mean, even after Adam and Eve sinned, God still made clothes for them and cared for them.

Those are great insights and reasonable critiques.

Well, I can see why Anselm's theory has been popular. It makes a lot of sense rationally, but I think the picture it offers of God is a little problematic, kind of cold and calculating instead of the passionate, loving God of the Bible.

I think you're right. In Anselm's scheme, divine justice totally trumps divine love. God *wants* to be loving, even sends the Son to be our substitute out of love. But God can't actually forgive us and restore the relationship with us until justice is served, payment is made, and someone's blood flows. Not only that, but the resurrection becomes almost totally superfluous.

Interesting. I'd pretty much forgotten about the resurrection, but I definitely don't see why it's needed. It seems like it's really Jesus' suffering and death that matter. Plus, when I think about it, I don't see how this really achieves "at-one-ment." I mean, yes, we're not condemned to die, but I don't really see how we're back in a good relationship with God.

That's a good point.

And I also don't see how this creates or even reflects the kingdom represented in Jesus' parables and teaching. According to Anselm, the father of the prodigal son is making a huge mistake. He should make someone pay before he lets the kid back home. So I think, in the end, Anselm's theory may be a great legal theory, but not such a hot relational one.

So maybe it's time to move on and see what's behind Door #2?

Yes indeed.

I think, given your reaction to Anselm, you might like this one a little better.

Good.

It was formulated by a guy who was born about fifty years after Anselm and, like you, didn't care for Anselm's cold legal rationality and the absence of God's love. His name was Peter Abelard.

Again with the A's!

Again with the A's.

Like I said, Abelard felt Anselm had sacrificed God's love to emphasize God's justice.

I'm with him!

So Abelard offered another explanation. In this story, the cross is not about payment or punishment but instead is the ultimate example of how much God loves us. Think again of John 3:16—"For God so loved the world that he gave his only Son. . . ."

The cross as the sign of God's love—I like that.
But how does that achieve atonement?

Abelard believed that when we saw God's tremendous love for us demonstrated on the cross, we would be so moved that we would want to love God back. Again, a verse associated with John serves as a rationale: "We love because God first loved us" (1 John 4:19).

So seeing God's love poured out on the cross moves us to love God. Okay, I can see that. But I'm still not sure how that deals with the problem of sin.

For Abelard, Jesus came both to show us God's love and to show us *how* to love others. He ended up being killed for that example, but when we saw how much he loved us, Abelard believed, we would not only love God in general but also love those around us, and in this way we would stop sinning and really *be* the children of God we were created to be.

So Jesus is primarily an example?

In a double sense: Jesus is an example of God's love, and Jesus is an example of how to love others. In fact, because of Abelard's emphasis on Jesus as example, his theory is sometimes called the "moral theory of atonement."

I can see that.

Okay, let me see if I've got this straight in relation to our three questions. It sounds like, according to Abelard, our problem is not so much sin itself as it is a lack of knowledge or motivation or both. That's why both of Jesus' examples work. He teaches us how to love as well as motivates us to do it.

I think that's fair.

God is easy. For Abelard, God is love, plain and simple.

But I'm still not totally sure how this achieves atonement. I guess the idea is that we are so caught up in love that we don't sin anymore. That at least sounds closer to the kingdom Jesus preached. But I'm just not sure I've ever seen that happen. Except maybe with Jesus, and that's kind of the point—we're not Jesus.

I mean, I love my family. But I still get mad at them. I still hurt them with my words and actions, sometimes by accident, for sure, but sometimes because I'm mad, or hurt, or afraid. So I'm not sure why Abelard thinks we'll do any better just because we see Jesus on the cross. Do you see what I mean?

Absolutely. I think these are all fair criticisms.

And while we're at it, why did Jesus have to die? Couldn't he have been an inspiring example without dying? Is death really the only thing that inspires us? I may not have liked Anselm's cold, bloody logic, but at least it was logical; at least it made sense. It feels like Anselm underestimates God's love, but Abelard underestimates human sin. I'm just not sure I buy his sense of how the cross really restores the relationship between us and God.

I'm inclined to agree with you.

And now that I think about it, what about the resurrection? You didn't mention that at all.

You're right; Abelard's theory, much like Anselm's, doesn't really do much of anything with the resurrection.

Then I think we should move on. Any more members of the A-Team waiting in the wings?

Well, as a matter of fact . . .

You've got to be kidding!

Not entirely. You see, the third theory we're going to talk about is actually the oldest, and it was championed by a number of early church theologians. But then it kind of dropped off the scene for about fifteen hundred years and was rediscovered and reintroduced to modern Christianity by a guy named Gustaf Aulén, a Swedish theologian with, indeed, a last name that begins with an "A."

Anselm, Abelard, and Aulén. Well, that shouldn't be hard to keep straight!

Don't feel bad if you get them confused. It happens all the time.

All right, I won't. So what did Aulén have to say?

His theory—or really I should say the theory that was popular in the early church—is a really interesting one, although it may sound a little odd to modern ears.

Let's hear it.

Okay, so it goes like this. The world has two great influences operating in it—one for good—God—and one for evil—the devil. Humanity is created by God to be good, but when Adam and Eve give in to the temptation of the serpent, who represents the devil, they betray their allegiance to God and so end up captive to the devil. This means that the devil has the ultimate claim upon their lives and destiny. So God, in the person of Jesus, offers himself as a ransom, like a trade, for humanity. The devil can't resist, because he knows if he can get hold of God's human Son, then he's essentially won the contest.

Here's where the Incarnation becomes so important. Jesus is God's human Son, but he is also divine. And because Jesus is divine as well as the human Son of God, and because he's innocent, Jesus can't be defeated, even by death. So when he is resurrected from the dead on Easter, he brings all of humanity—no longer captive to the devil—with him.

Well, I'll say one thing for Aulén, he's got style! This is really quite imaginative.

Yeah, although it's important to recognize that Aulén was mostly reminding the modern church—he wrote about all this in the 1930s and '40s—of what the ancient church taught. And in the ancient world there was a very strong sense of the active presence of the devil, whose greatest power was to inflict death. So defeating death, way more than paying the penalty for sin, was a huge concern.

So did Jesus trick the devil? Is that what Aulén and company think went on?

There is an element of deception, but it's less like a trick and more like the disguise one might wear to penetrate enemy territory. In the Incarnation Jesus takes on human form, which the devil believes he can defeat, and so attacks him in death. But the devil doesn't count on Jesus being divine and doesn't take account of his innocence, and so unwittingly gives Jesus the opening to defeat the devil and death itself.

It reminds me a little of Star Wars. You know, the scene where Obi-Wan Kenobi says to Darth Vader something like, "If you strike me down, I will become more powerful than you can imagine." And that's what happens. Darth Vader can't resist, but by killing Obi-Wan in the body, he releases him to aid Luke in the ultimate victory over evil.

Yeah, that's not a bad parallel.

How does Aulén's theory answer our three questions?

It's a little more challenging with Aulén, but I'll give it a try: First, our problem is that we were fooled by the serpent and sinned. Because of that we are now held captive by death and the devil.

Second, God's primary characteristic is . . . hmm . . . this is where it gets difficult. I guess I would say that God is the one who loves us enough to enter into the human condition and suffer death for our sake.

And third, this achieves atonement because it frees us from the claims of the devil, takes away the fear of death—which Jesus has defeated—and opens up our future with God.

This reminds me of a book I've read to my sister's kids, C. S. Lewis's *The Lion, the Witch, and the Wardrobe*. Have you read it?

You bet.

Then you'll remember that Aslan the lion, who is kind of the Jesus-figure in the story, obeys the deep magic that gives the White Witch claim to Edmund, a disobedient "son of Adam." But then she forgets the deeper magic that says that when an innocent life is traded, death itself is broken. So Aslan comes back from death and defeats her.

I think you're right. That's a very good example of this theory of atonement. Perhaps because it portrays the cross and resurrection as a cosmic battle between good and evil, this theory has inspired a lot of art and literature through the ages.

So, I'm curious, what do you think?

Well, it's nice for someone to take the resurrection seriously. I mean, up to now no one has done that. And I can see how the emphasis on victory—over death, the devil, all that stuff—would be appealing.

But . . .

But it's a little too far out for me to take seriously. I just don't think the ancient emphasis on the devil and God's need to disguise Jesus can really speak to our age. I actually do think there's something powerful about the idea that Jesus enters into our life and takes on our condition in order to struggle with and defeat death. Struggle is very much what I feel like when it comes to my dad's cancer. You know? It's a real fight. And I like the idea of God also fighting these things that hold us captive.

But at the same time it feels like it gets a little too symbolic. I mean, I don't see why the devil should have a claim on us in the first place. Who made that rule? God? Then why can't God just change it without all the drama? And what does any of this have to do with the kingdom Jesus preaches?

> I can understand what you mean. The theory Aulén champions was fashioned at a time when people viewed the world in very different terms than we do now.

So I guess it's three up and three down. Struck out. But is there any way we could combine elements of all three?

> Interesting. Which parts would you take?

Well, I think Anselm takes human sin really seriously. It's not something we can just get over if we're motivated enough, as in Abelard, and it's not some part of a cosmic game, as it feels like in Aulén. It's real, and it's really a problem.

But I also love Abelard's emphasis on God's love. That seems to fit the God we've been talking about better than Anselm's idea of a God so committed to justice that no forgiveness is possible apart from punishment.

And I love the sense of struggle and victory that Aulén describes.

So . . . do you think we could just combine the best parts of all three and blend them together?

> Sort of an atonement smoothie?

Exactly what the doctor called for! What do you think?

> Well, I definitely agree with you that there are parts of each of these three theories that are appealing. But I suspect that we aren't going to be satisfied by posing one more theory, even a theory that chooses from the best parts of the other three.

That's right; I forgot. You don't like theories very much.

For some things—like physics or economics—theories are just fine, even very helpful. These are things you can study in a relatively detached kind of way. But a theory of love, or of a relationship? It's not the same thing at all. I mean, imagine if your significant other asks, "Do you love me?" and you answer, "Let me share with you my theory about love." How do you think that would go over?

Not well at all. Yeah, I see what you mean. If our problem is an out-of-whack relationship with God, then no *theory* about atonement, which is essentially about restoring relationships, is going to work.

I think that's right. Theories are good at offering a snapshot of something. At their best they can even describe and predict behavior, but they can't actually create the experience being described.

It's one thing to go over a theory with your six year-old about how to ride a bike. It's another to get on and start pedaling.

Exactly.

So what do you suggest?

That we take more seriously the actual accounts in the Bible about what led up to Jesus' crucifixion, including the kind of kingdom he proclaims, and then also look to see how his disciples experienced his resurrection. By paying attention to the details of the story, we might see something different, something that actually has an effect on us and on our relationship with God.

Sounds good. Where do we start?

Same place we started our conversation in general.

With creation and original blessing?

Right, with original blessing and also original insecurity.

Which brings us to the human condition or problem—sin. Can I give this a try?

Sure.

In a general sense we're agreeing with Anselm about sin. But sin isn't so much an offense to God's honor or justice. It's more that we do all kinds of things that hurt ourselves and each other because of the insecurity and confusion that are part of the human condition. We use people and love things, we assert ourselves over others, we establish or maintain a pecking order, we try to know and control the future, and so on.

Very well put. And in all these ways we try to overcome or escape our creaturely dependence on God and establish ourselves on our own.

Okay. And with Abelard the character of God is love, the love that infused God's creation.

Right again. Tenacious, parental, sacrificial love.

Sacrificial? That sounds like Anselm.

Well, one way to talk about sacrifice is to think about the kind of sacrifice we need to make to satisfy God's anger. That's the way Anselm thought about it. But another way to think about it is to point to the sacrifice that God makes for us, in this case stressing God's sacrificial love. That is, according to the biblical witness, God would do anything, sacrifice anything, in order to communicate God's love to us. Like any parent would.

Got it. But what exactly does this have to do with Jesus' death? And how does all this contribute to our relationship with God being restored?

The clash of these two things—our original insecurity and sin and God's tenacious love—furnishes the essential plotline of the Bible. Think about it: If you wanted to reduce the plotline of the Old Testament to a sentence, what would you write?

Hmm. How about this: "God created us in love to be in relationship with each other and God, but we keep running from God, trying to make it on our own, and do great harm to ourselves and each other in the process."

That's very good.

Can I have another sentence?

Sure.

Then here goes: "Every time we run, God comes after us with covenant and law, with warning and judgment, with judges, kings, and prophets; but while that may help for a while, in the end we still run and hide, preferring to be on our own and alone rather than in relationship with—and in that sense dependent on—God."
Well, how'd I do?

Long sentence, but I think you did a fabulous job.

Thanks.

You're welcome. I think you've not only got the basic plot of the Old Testament down, but you've also described our predicament as sinful human beings. And that will be important when we try to see how God deals with it. In three of the Gospels, Jesus offers a similar summary in another one of his parables. I'll tell you ahead of time, it didn't go over all that well with his audience.

I'd like to hear it.

I'll share Matthew's version, where Jesus is debating some of the religious rulers and says:

> "Listen to another parable. There was a landowner who planted a vineyard, put a fence around it, dug a wine press in it, and built a watchtower. Then he leased it to tenants and went to another country. When the harvest time had come, he sent his slaves to the tenants to collect his produce. But the tenants seized his slaves and beat one, killed another, and stoned another. Again he sent other slaves, more than the first; and they treated them in the same way. Finally he sent his son to them, saying, 'They will respect my son.' But when the tenants saw the son, they said to themselves, 'This is the heir; come, let us kill him and get his inheritance.' So they seized him, threw him out of the vineyard, and killed him. Now when the owner of the vineyard comes, what will he do to those tenants?" They said to him, "He will put those wretches to a miserable death, and lease the vineyard to other tenants who will give him the produce at the harvest time." (Matthew 21:33-41)

Wow. That really is it in a nutshell. The servants are obviously the prophets and the son of the landowner is Jesus, so it's the history not only of Israel but also of Jesus. What I don't understand, though, is why the tenants thought they would inherit the vineyard. It seems a little crazy.

That's hard to tell. It may be that they thought that if the son was coming, that meant the landowner was dead. So if they kill the heir, then they can claim the vineyard as their own. After all, they've been working it all these years, so they would have a legal right to claim it if no heir was left.

It still seems a little crazy. Though, when I think about it, not as crazy as the landowner.

What do you mean?

Well, here is this landowner who sends servant after servant only to have them beaten, stoned, and killed. And then he sends his son?! What kind of nut is he? I mean, why in the world does he think that after all that has happened they might respect his son?

That's a really important point. And I think it gets at the heart of the gospel. God loves us so much that, like a desperate parent, there is nothing that God won't try to win us back, even when it seems a little crazy.

That brings us back to my—and I guess most people's—favorite Bible verse, John 3:16: "For God so loved the world that he gave his only Son, so that everyone who believes in him may not perish but may have eternal life."

Yeah, it really is a great verse, what Martin Luther called "the gospel in a nutshell." But do you know what comes right after it?

No, what?

Jesus continues what he's saying:

> *Indeed, God did not send the Son into the world to condemn the world, but in order that the world might be saved through him. Those who believe in him are not condemned; but those who do not believe are condemned already, because they have not believed in the name of the only Son of God. And this is the judgment, that the light has come into*

the world, and people loved darkness rather than light because their deeds were evil. For all who do evil hate the light and do not come to the light, so that their deeds may not be exposed. (John 3:17-20)

Boy, it's almost exactly what we've been saying. God loves the world, but the world runs away.

But I'm still not sure I understand how this relates to our discussion of the atonement. I mean, what does this have to do with why Jesus dies and is raised again, and how does it restore our relationship with God?

There are two parts to the answer to that question. Or maybe I should say the cross and resurrection *do* two things to us to heal and restore our relationship with God.

They *do* two things to us?

Yes. This is why I want to get beyond *theories* of atonement, so we can actually focus on the *event* of atonement, on something actually *happening* to us.

Okay, then what's the first thing the cross and resurrection do?

To get at that, let's go back to the biblical story. You did a great job summarizing the Old Testament story. I'd like to try the same with the New.

Sounds good.

Okay, here it is: Jesus comes to town proclaiming the kingdom of God by preaching, teaching, doing miracles to feed and heal people, and forgiving sins, and he gets killed for it.

Okay, I know we've talked in general about how humanity runs from God, but it gets a little harder to understand when you describe Jesus' ministry this concretely. It just doesn't seem like something you'd get killed for. Don't most people want food, healing, and forgiveness?

I'd agree that most people want food and healing.

What about forgiveness? Don't most people want that, too?

Good point. Okay, I forgive you.

Wait a second—what in the world did I do?!

What does it matter? Didn't you just say that most people want for-giveness? I figured you were like most people, so I forgave you.

Yeah, but come on, I didn't do anything.

So?

So? Well, if I didn't do anything, then who are you to forgive me?

Exactly.

Ah . . . I think I see what you mean. Forgiveness is great if you want it, if you know you did something wrong. But if not, it's just plain offensive, like you're accusing me of something. That's why Jesus' parables about God's kingdom made some people mad.

And that's the pattern we see repeated over and over again in the Bible. It's right there in John's Gospel: God loved the world and so sent his Son, the light of the world, but the people ran from the light. And it's right there in Matthew: The landowner sent his son because he wanted to reach out to the tenants. He thought they would respect him, but they just kill him. Read the Gospels and it happens over and over again. The people who know they've messed up, who know they are caught in sin, gratefully accept Jesus' promise of forgiveness. But the ones who believe they are righteous on their own—the ones in power—find Jesus' words offensive and put him to death.

So the cross was their way, as John writes, of hating and fleeing the light because their deeds were evil. Or, to put it another way, just by offering them forgiveness Jesus made them look bad, so they put him to death.

Right. The cross shows us what happens when God, the one who is perfectly good and holy, comes to earth, even in love. And truth be told, we'd still rather run away from this God or, if worse comes to worst, get rid of this God, than admit that we're broken, sinful, and in need of forgiveness.

Sounds like Adam and Eve hiding when they heard the Lord walking in the garden. Of course, Adam and Eve thought they were going to get in trouble. Do you think this is true even when God comes offering forgiveness?

You saw for yourself, unless you have some deep sense that you need forgiveness, someone offering it feels more like an accusation than help. In this way we're no different than Adam and Eve. Admitting our need for God, our need for forgiveness, our need for anything beyond our control, is terrifying. It feels like dying, and so we run away.

I think I understand a little better now what you meant about not wanting another *theory* of the atonement but instead wanting to focus on what actually *happens* when confronted by the cross, by Jesus and his forgiveness.

Say a little more.

Well, when you said you forgave me, it actually made me mad. It had an *effect* on me. Which makes me think that I probably wouldn't have reacted any differently to Jesus when he came in the first century. Unless I somehow realized that I was sinful, that I had repeatedly missed the mark, I probably would have found Jesus offensive, too. So I can see how Jesus' words of forgiveness—not to mention his preaching of a new kingdom where we're all equal—would be threatening, and how they still are. They threaten to take away the control we try so hard to keep by making us dependent on God's mercy. It's downright maddening.

And that's the first thing the cross actually *does* to us. It makes us experience the truth about our fear and insecurity, about our desire to be in control, about how there's almost anything we'd rather do than admit our deep need, the great big God-shaped hole that all humans have and none of us can fill on our own. And this truth puts to death all of our dreams of making it on our own.

It's like God just stands there, looks us right in the eye, and says, "Look. I know you. I know deep down just who you are." And when God says that, it's just no use running, hiding, or pretending anymore. The jig is up. And suddenly all of our little dreams, schemes, and contingency plans just vanish, curl into smoke.

Frankly, that's a little painful.

After all we've talked about so far, did you imagine that restoring our relationship with God would be easy?

Good point. In fact, I guess I should be a little suspicious if you offered me any easy formula for atonement.

Okay, so what's the second thing Jesus' cross and resurrection do to us?

The first thing the cross and resurrection do is to put to death our dreams of independence by telling us the truth about ourselves. The second thing the cross and resurrection do is to restore our relationship with God—or really to create a new relationship—by telling us the truth about God's response to us.

And what *is* God's response?

Let's start with what we expect it to be. You know, how do you think God will respond? How do you think God *should* respond after all of our running and hiding and after we end up putting God's Son to death rather than give up control and accept his forgiveness?

Actually, I think it was there in the parable of Jesus you shared a couple of minutes ago. You know, "He will put those wretches to a miserable death, and lease the vineyard to other tenants who will give him the produce at the harvest time." I mean, it's a little weird saying that, because it sounds more like Anselm's God of punishment than Abelard's God of love, but it sure feels like what we should expect. We've really screwed up.

But I guess that's not what happens, is it?

No. Keep in mind that while Jesus asks the question, it's the religious authorities who answer. And I think their answer pretty much reflects the world's way of dealing with this kind of problem.

What do you mean?

I think that out of our insecurity, we've learned to trust only what we can count and control. That's why Anselm's theory is so popular; it reduces sin to an accounting problem. If there's sin, there must be punishment. That's the way Anselm saw it, and that's the way the religious authorities saw it. The tenants broke the law, violated the terms of the relationship, and must now be punished.

But that's not the way God deals with it.

Right. In the verse from John 3 that we looked at earlier, Jesus answers differently: "God did *not* send the Son into the world to condemn the world, but in order that the world might be saved through him."

Why? Because God so *loved* the world. Not "held the world accountable," not "wanted to forgive the world but couldn't." No, it's "for God so loved the world"—the *whole* world, including *us*, including you and me and everyone else who would have put God's Son to death rather than accept the forgiveness that is so frightening we'd rather kill than give up control to receive it.

So it's love all the way through. It's love that does both things.

Say a little more.

Well, let's start with the first truth. First, God comes in love—like that crazy landlord—offering us forgiveness and restoring us to new relationship. And that frightens us, but eventually it also kills us, shows us the truth about who we are, a truth we can't escape or avoid unless we're going to live in complete denial. And then when God's love is done showing us the truth of how sinful we are, even when that truth has made us so mad we'd like to get rid of God, it's still there. God's love is still right in front of us, promising never to go away. So we kind of wake up and realize the second truth, that God still loves us, has always loved us.

And what does that realization, that second truth, *do* to you?

Are you kidding? It makes me feel alive again, like everything is new, like anything and everything is possible—including being in relationship with God.

Which might be what the apostle Paul means when he says that when we die with Christ we also are raised to new life in Christ (Romans 6:5-8). The two truths God tells us in Jesus really do both put us to death and raise us to new life.

Is that how it works, then? God first tells us God knows us, so we stop hiding and pretending and just give up. And then God tells us God loves us, just as we are. Is that how it works?

What do you think?

I think it feels like God's love first drives us a little crazy, a little beyond ourselves. And then God's love, the same love, brings us back and makes everything new again. Yes, I think that through Jesus' cross and resurrection God says to us, "I know you *and* I love you."

I do, too. And that's what we see in Jesus—in his preaching and teaching, in his feeding and healing, and in welcoming *everyone* to be in relationship with him.

Yeah, I can see that.

It's even in the very fact of his incarnation.

What do you mean?

Just that when God takes on our human flesh to restore our relationship, God is saying that anyone—*anyone* who is part of the human race, including the people we don't like or we think we're better than—is still loved by God.

And so that's where it all comes together—the Incarnation, the new kingdom Jesus preaches and models, and his death and resurrection. They're all part of the two truths that God tells us out of love.

And both truths really matter.

No kidding. We want the love, but we won't trust it unless we really know God loves us. Isn't that our lives in a nutshell? We want to be loved, but we

can't trust the person who says "I love you" unless they really know us. Otherwise, they might just love the person we're pretending to be. And we're afraid that if they find out who we really are, they might run away. So we're caught: we want love, but we're afraid that if we let other people really know us, they might reject us. That's why God's "I *know* you" matters so much.

Right.

But if that's all God said, we'd be no better off. So God also says—or really has been saying all along but now we can finally hear it—"I love you." And the "I know you" and the "I love you" together create a new possibility.

I think you're exactly right. And that's why the resurrection is so important. It's not just that the cross forces us to see and feel these things; the resurrection does too. I mean, the cross is the symbol of God's profound love—it shows us just how far God will go and just how much God will endure to tell us that God loves us. But the resurrection shows us that love wins, that life wins, that God's love is more powerful than death and that the God who created heaven and earth in the first place can create new life.

I guess if God raised Jesus from the dead, then God can restore me, too.

Exactly. The apostle Paul once wrote that "if anyone is in Christ, there is a new creation: everything old has passed away; see, everything has become new!" (2 Corinthians 5:17). And this is not just about a single new thing, or even just a single new person. It's about total newness—new life, new opportunity, new relationship, a whole new world.

Yeah, that's it. That's totally it. That's at-one-ment. We die, or give up, or relent, or whatever, and then we find new life, new relationship, a new world, and all the rest. That's cool, very cool.

But I've still got a question: What about sin?

What about sin?

Well, what happens to it? You know, Anselm's question. How does God deal with our sin?

God forgives us.

God just forgives us? But how can God do that? What about God's honor and justice and all that?

My goodness, but you suddenly sound a lot like Anselm.

Oh, I know I do, and I can't say I like it. But it still seems like an important question. I mean, we've taken sin very seriously, and all of a sudden it seems like no big deal.

Sin is a very big deal; you're right. But keep in mind your own reaction to Anselm's solution—you said it might work well in the legal court but not so hot in a relationship. And I think you're right. If we define sin primarily as the individual bad things we do all of our lives, then the problem is how to clear our divine balance sheet of all those sins so we can approach God again.

But we've said sin is not only or even primarily about individual deeds. It is more about our condition of insecurity and fear that drives us away from God, and our fundamental problem is that our relationship with God has been damaged. In that case, I don't see what's wrong with God coming to us and forgiving us. It's a different way to deal with sin, because it defines the central issue not as an accounting problem but as a relational one. Paul says as much in the verses just after the one about a new creation: "All this is from God, who reconciled us to himself through Christ" (2 Corinthians 5:18).

You know, it's funny how easy it is to get caught up thinking that atonement means focusing on God, focusing on what needs to happen for God to love us again. I guess Paul is saying that the problem was actually with us. It's God reconciling *us*.

Right. At another place, Paul writes, "God proves his love for us in that while we still were sinners Christ died for us" (Romans 5:8).

God didn't wait for us. God just went ahead and loved us and forgave us. When you think about it, that's kind of audacious.

And maybe just what you'd expect from the God of the Bible.

I think you're right.
    So I think we've done it.

Done what?

Come up with a pretty good atonement smoothie. I mean, we've taken sin seriously, with Anselm. We're all about God's love, with Abelard. And the resurrection is the promise that God's love is victorious, which we've borrowed from Aulén. It really is all here.

Except . . .

Except not as a theory, but as an actual event. Atonement is something that happens in our real life that restores, actually re-creates, our relationship with God.

> That's what it's all about: creation and new creation, sin and forgiveness, death and new life, cross and resurrection.

And in the end, God's love wins. God's desire to be in relationship with us is stronger than our desire to go it alone. Love wins.

Love wins.

And so life wins, too.

In the end, life wins, too.

Which means that with the promise of new life in Christ, we win, too—all of us. Very cool.

Insights and Questions

The 2 truths about the
Cross & resurrection.
1. We ~~can~~ can stop hiding
and pretending we know things
because God knows us.
2. God tells us he loves
us (all people) just the way
we are. (forgiveness)
Our dreams of independence
are put to death and
our relationship with God is
restored because we have
a new relationship.

CHAPTER 7

The Body of Christ
Church and Holy Spirit

So how are you doing?

How do you mean?

Well, we just covered an enormous amount of material, some of it pretty intense, so I was wondering how you're doing processing it all.

That's a good question. It's a lot to absorb. I think that will take some time. But I am encouraged, even excited, about the story we're talking about. It can be pretty intense, even dark at times, but it's also really uplifting—to think that God would come after us and keep after us until we recognize just how much God loves us.

God's love is definitely at the heart of the biblical story.

And it's not only that. I was surprised that it's not only about experiencing God's love in the present, but also about how God's love affects the way we think about the future.

Say a little more.

I'll try. I'm just thinking it through now, but it feels like the cross shows us just how much God loves us. It demonstrates that there's nothing we *have done*—no insecurity, fear, confusion, or sin—that would make God turn away from us. But it's also, in a way, about the future, because we know that there's nothing we *can do* in the future that will make God stop loving us either. Then comes the resurrection, and that feels almost totally about the future. It's not only that God loves us, but that God's love is more powerful than death. So the resurrection promises that death doesn't have the last word, that it's not the last page of the story.

That's very insightful, and I think right on the mark. Winston Churchill's funeral witnessed to this same conviction.

Churchill, as in the British prime minister from World War II?

That's the one. He was a Christian and planned his own funeral in almost every detail. A lot of it was very similar to most Christian funerals, but at the very end of the service, a solitary bugler stood at the west end of St. Paul's Cathedral and played taps, the song of the evening and the end of the day. Taps is the song the military plays to mark a death and to signal their mourning.

That was probably very moving.

I'm sure it was. But then, after a long moment's silence, another bugler stood up at the other end of the cathedral, on the east where the sun rises. He played reveille, the song of the morning, the song of a new day and of victory.

That totally captures it! After taps and evening, there's reveille and the promise of a new day. After death there's new life.

Yeah, that's it in a nutshell.
Do you mind if I ask you another question?

Not at all.

I'm wondering how all this influences the way you've been thinking about some of the questions you brought—questions about your friend, your dad, and whether God's worth believing in.

You know, I was just thinking about that myself. On the one hand, I feel like some pieces are beginning to fall into place. I appreciate the idea of God caring for all of us so much, of feeling our sorrow and pain. That feels like part of the promise of the Incarnation. And it helps to remember what we were just talking about—that part of the promise of the cross and resurrection is that whatever may happen here, there's still a new day waiting.

And on the other hand?

On the other hand, it's still hard.

Can you say a little more?

It's just that knowing about these promises is one thing, and believing them is another. Do you know what I mean?

I think so. You've named two of the central promises of the Christian faith. In the Incarnation, God promises to be with us through all of our ups and downs in this life. And in the cross and resurrection, God promises to stay with us and to bring us through life and death to new life. I think what you're saying is that thinking about these things is helpful, and understanding them is even more helpful. But sometimes, actually believing them can be more challenging. And while understanding is nice, it's believing them that makes a real difference.

Exactly. And it's not that I don't believe them. Sometimes it all feels very real and very hopeful. At other times, though, it's just hard to believe. I guess what's frustrating is that I started this conversation with all kinds of questions and doubts. And although I feel like I've learned a lot and believe more, I still have questions and doubts. Does that mean that I just don't have much faith? Or if I'm a Christian, maybe I'm just not a very good one?

Actually, I'd say that having doubts and questions even after learning a lot about the faith—maybe *especially* after learning about the faith—makes you a perfectly normal Christian.

Really? I mean, shouldn't you have fewer questions as you become a better Christian?

Only if being a Christian is about knowing certain information, about being able to pass a final exam or write a term paper about the essential Christian doctrines. But we've been talking about a God who's interested in being in relationship with us. And relationships always have ups and downs. They involve as much mystery as they do knowledge, and they include doubt as well as faith. Think about any meaningful relationship you've been in—with your friend, with your parents and siblings, with classmates or coworkers—and you know that they don't just keep sailing along, getting better and better every day in each and every way.

That's definitely true, but I guess I thought that as I came to know and believe more, I'd question less.

I don't think you're alone in that assumption. In fact, I suspect there are two very different ways of thinking about the Christian faith. And one of them is just what you're describing.

What do you mean?

Both ways of thinking about the Christian faith recognize that this world is a turbulent place, filled with challenges and obstacles, all kinds of ups and downs. One view assumes that once you come to faith, all the tremors—the doubts, questions, challenges, and the like—*stop*. The other way to think about the Christian faith is to believe that faith helps you keep your footing *amid* the tremors.

That's interesting, and it helps me a little to stop feeling bad about having all these questions and doubts.

> Absolutely. Keep in mind that all the accounts of the resurrection in the New Testament begin with stories of the disbelief and doubts of the disciples. Questions and doubts, as I've said before, are the marks of a lively and engaged faith. It's not doubt you have to worry about; it's disinterest, whether you're not interested because you just don't care or because you think you already know everything.

Again, that's helpful. But it makes me want to go back to one of the things we said before.

> What's that?

Well, we talked about Adam and Eve—really, all of us—having a God-shaped hole, you know, a sense of our need and insufficiency. We often try to fill that hole with all kinds of things instead of with a relationship with God.

> Yeah, that was a big part of our conversation about sin. Sin is, in a sense, thinking you can overcome that need on your own, by achieving or buying or owning or whatever.

Right. But the way we talked about it makes it seem like once you come to faith, once you develop a relationship with God, then God fills that hole and it goes away. And maybe some people experience it that way. Maybe that's part of that first way of thinking about faith. But the second way—faith helping you keep your footing amid the tremors—makes me think that God doesn't just fill the hole once and for all.

> You know, I think you're probably right. I've found talking about the God-shaped hole helpful in terms of describing the general condition of humanity, our "original insecurity," but I don't think I realized how easily that could play into a sense that Christian faith should remove that hole, that insecurity, once and for all. That's incredibly helpful.

I'm really glad you think so. It feels a little more realistic to me to talk about it that way. But that opens up another question: How do we get by in the meantime? How do we not get totally stuck in our questions and doubts? I guess if faith doesn't remove all the tremors, then I'm asking *how* faith helps

us keep our footing amid them, especially when sometimes it feels so very hard just to believe.

That's a fantastic question. And I think the best way we can get at it is to talk about the Holy Spirit and the church.

Hmm.

What?

Well, I guess it's easier for me to imagine talking about the church than the Holy Spirit. The church is a thing—you know, an institution that you can see and feel and describe. But the Holy Spirit? I don't know, maybe I've just been around my sister too much, but it seems that for a lot of Christians *everything* is the Holy Spirit—good things that happen, bad things that happen, the weather, vacation plans. I've never quite been able to understand what they mean when they talk about it.

That's a fair concern. The Holy Spirit can be a complicated topic, especially in our modern world where we don't talk much about "spirit" at all, or at least not like people used to in the ancient world the Bible came from. But I think we can talk about the Holy Spirit in a way that makes some sense, and you actually just pointed the way.

If so, it wasn't on purpose!

It's when you mentioned how talking about the church seemed easier than talking about the Holy Spirit. Christians have regularly connected these two things, believing that the Holy Spirit works in and through the church. Or, to put it another way, that the church is the way the Holy Spirit is made visible in the world.

I'm not sure I'm following.

Understandable. Like I said, this can be complicated at first. It might help to turn again to some passages from the Bible.

It usually seems to.

Okay, so there are two places I think we can start. The first is in John's Gospel, on the eve of the crucifixion when Jesus is preparing his disciples for the time when he will leave them. To help them get ready to carry on their mission when he's no longer physically present with them, he talks about the coming of the Holy Spirit, who he describes as a counselor and an advocate who will help the disciples remember his teaching when he is gone (John 16:4-15).

So that's what the Holy Spirit does—help us remember Jesus and what he taught?

Remember and believe. Yes. In that sense, the Holy Spirit is the ongoing presence of Jesus with us. But the Spirit is also the one who draws us together into the church, gathers us together into a people who share a common story—the story of God's mission to bless and save the whole world—and helps us believe that story, helps us to make it our own.

To get a better idea of the part of the story that deals with the Holy Spirit and the church, it'll be helpful to turn to the story of Pentecost in Acts.

Acts?

The Acts of the Apostles. It's written by the same person who wrote the Gospel of Luke. In fact, Acts is the second half of Luke's two-part history: the first part is about Jesus, and the second is about the church.

And Pentecost?

The name *Pentecost* means "fifty days." It was originally a Jewish harvest festival that drew Jewish believers to the temple in Jerusalem from all over the ancient world. In Luke's story, Jesus told the disciples to wait in Jerusalem until they were given the Holy Spirit.

Was that in the Gospel of Luke or Acts?

Both, actually. That scene functions as a bridge between the two stories. The Gospel of Luke ends with Jesus promising the disciples that they will be "clothed with power from on high" (24:49), and then Acts starts with the same promise, this time with Jesus saying that the disciples will be "baptized with the Holy Spirit" (1:5). And that's what happens when the disciples are gathered together in Jerusalem on Pentecost, which happens to be fifty days after Jesus' resurrection.

The Holy Spirit comes upon them like the rush of a mighty wind and looks like tongues of fire descending on them, and suddenly they are given the courage to preach the story of Jesus to everyone who had come to the festival. Everyone who hears them understands what the disciples are saying in their own language, and three thousand people come to faith and are baptized.

I'd say that does look like being clothed with power from on high. I mean, that's a lot of people!

Which is why most Christians regard Pentecost as the day the church was born.

And you said that everyone understood what the disciples were saying, even though they came from different countries and spoke different languages.

That's the way Luke describes it, which actually gives us a clue to what the church is.

Oh?

Yeah. We might say that, first and foremost, the church exists wherever the story of Jesus is preached and heard so that people come to faith, all with the help of the Holy Spirit.

So the church isn't a place?

No, not really. I mean, the church definitely occupies distinct places—like the local congregation where your friends had their baby baptized. And in one sense, as you said, the church is an institution that you can see, feel, and describe. But in another sense, it isn't so much a building or an institution as it is a *people*, a community joined by their belief in Jesus. I think this is what the story Luke tells is principally about.

So God is forming another community gathered around a new promise, just like Abraham and his descendants were gathered around the earlier promise of the covenant.

That's right. In fact, Christians call that part of the Bible that contains the story of Jesus and the early church the New "Testament," which is another word for "covenant."

So there's a new covenant that is connected with the old. And there's a new community, which is also connected to the old, that we call the church.

Right.

Do people still hear the gospel in different languages today, even when it's preached in one language?

I've only ever understood sermons that were preached in English, but I think Luke is making a larger confession of faith that will be helpful to our discussion about the church.

Fire away.

Well, I think Luke is saying that Pentecost is the reverse of the Tower of Babel story.

Remind me of that one.

Sure. In Genesis all the people of the world speak one language. They decide to build a tower large enough to climb up into the heavens, but God decides to give them different languages so they can't finish it.

Why in the world does God do that?

That's a great question. It may be that this story is similar to the tree of knowledge story earlier in Genesis, that humans are reaching beyond themselves in an attempt to be completely independent from God. Or it may be that, once again, Genesis is offering a story that describes the way things are, more than it is trying to explain scientifically how things came to be.

That's always helpful to remember.
So you were saying that Pentecost reverses Babel.

Yes. I think so. At Babel everyone spoke the same language and then had their languages confused. But now at Pentecost the Holy Spirit makes it possible for all these different people, despite their distinctive languages, to hear and understand the gospel.

And Luke's confession of faith in this is . . . ?

That Pentecost inaugurates a new beginning, the start of a new humanity and new community. This community is linked not by their biological relationship but through their shared belief that, in Jesus, God is keeping all the promises and covenants God made with Israel so as to bless the whole world.

And the Holy Spirit makes all this happen?

That's what Christians confess—that the Holy Spirit created, and actually still creates, the church to bear witness to God's promises.

"Still creates." So the Holy Spirit is still at work, even though we don't see it? I mean, you don't often hear about mighty winds or tongues of fire.

Right, and that's important. We may experience the Spirit in powerful, dramatic ways, but we may also often experience the Spirit's presence in subtler things like the sharing of the story of Jesus or acts of mercy, love, and kindness. Christians confess that it's the Spirit who actually motivates and empowers us to do these things.

It sounds like we're back to the two kinds of relationships God values. God wants to be in relationship with us, and the church helps with that by telling the story of Jesus. And God wants us to be in relationship with each other, and the church helps by encouraging us to do these acts of mercy, love, and kindness.

Very much so.

I have to say it's easier for me to see how the church takes care of the first relationship between God and us—telling the story of Jesus. But when it comes to the second one—our relationships with each other through acts of mercy and kindness—how does the church influence that?

Two ways. First, the church encourages, instructs, and equips individual members to share God's love through what they say and do, and not just to each other but to everyone. Do you remember when we were discussing covenant and community and we mentioned that Jesus was once asked to summarize the law?

Sure. He said that the most important laws were to love God and to love your neighbor.

Right. After that, someone asks him, "Who is my neighbor?" In response, Jesus tells the parable of the Good Samaritan (Luke 10:25-37).

I recognize that parable. It's about helping others, isn't it?

Yes, although there's a bit of a twist to the story. Someone gets hurt while traveling. Two religious leaders come down the same road but cross over to the other side to avoid him. Then along comes a Samaritan who helps the man, takes him to an inn, and then pays the innkeeper to make sure the man is well cared for. The Samaritan is Jesus' example of the kind of person who fulfills the law. What gives the parable some bite is that Samaritans were an ethnic minority and considered seriously inferior by most Jews at the time.

So if a Samaritan recognizes who your neighbor is, we all should.

Exactly—your neighbor is anyone who is in need. Anyone. Period.

Okay, so the church encourages Christians to help anyone who is in need. What's the second way the church helps care for our relationships with each other?

The church not only encourages us to work as individuals but also organizes as a community to help. So some churches might run soup kitchens, while others staff a homeless shelter. Some will band

together to build a hospital, while others will advocate to the govern
ment for better programs to help people who are struggling.

The church is involved in advocacy?

Absolutely. Christians confess that God is at work in the world in all
kinds of ways, and that includes through government, so the church
can advocate on behalf of those who may not have much of a voice
otherwise. Across the centuries, the church has helped millions of
poor people, organized social institutions like orphanages and hos-
pitals, even spoken out against tyrants.

Really?

Really. A group of German theologians, for instance, opposed Hit-
ler's claim to be God's divine agent in the 1930s and '40s.

What happened to them?

Some of them were forced out of the country. Others were rounded
up and put in prison. Some died, but others survived to tell their
story. More recently, the church has played a role in helping to heal
the racial division in South Africa. Archbishop Desmond Tutu, a
prominent Christian who worked for the end of apartheid, chaired
the Truth and Reconciliation Commission that has been so important there.

I guess I didn't know the church was so politically involved.

The point isn't to take one political side or another, but to work with
governments to help take care of all the people of God, in the church
and beyond it. And it's not just governments that we see God working through, but all kinds of agencies, institutions, and other faith
communities. And that means that we can partner with, encourage,
and support all kinds of people to care for this world.

Even if they don't believe in God, or believe in a different god?

Christians confess that *anytime* you see someone—whether a person, an agency, or a faith community—helping care for other people
and creation, you are seeing the influence of the God who created
and still loves all people and the world.

And you're saying that this is also the work of the Holy Spirit? I mean, I know lots of people who aren't Christians do acts of mercy, love, and kindness. I guess I just didn't expect you to say that it was the Holy Spirit.

Earlier I said that the Holy Spirit works in and through the church. That's different, though, than saying the Holy Spirit can *only* work through the church.

But I thought, since we're talking about the Christian church, that was kind of assumed.

On the one hand, I think that's a fair assumption. And when it comes to sharing the gospel, then I'd say that's definitely the Holy Spirit at work through the church. On the other hand, in John's Gospel Jesus compares the Spirit to wind which "blows where it chooses" (John 3:8). So Christians believe that the Holy Spirit involves us in two key ways. The Holy Spirit helps us do the work of sharing the good news of what God has accomplished in Jesus, but also helps us—and all people—with the original work God gave us in caring for the whole world.

You mean the work God gave to Adam and Eve as part of God's original blessing? You know, to be partners with God in caring for each other and the world?

Right. Some of the work God gives us is what we might call distinctively Christian—sharing the story of Jesus. But some of it—the second kind dealing with caring for each other—is done by all kinds of people, even people who don't believe in Jesus. And that makes sense, because the God who raised Jesus from the dead is also the one who created the whole world and everyone in it in the first place.

So it sounds like the Holy Spirit is bigger than the church, or at least can't be contained in the church?

I think God is always bigger than what we can imagine, and that includes God the Holy Spirit being bigger than the church.

Then why do we need the church at all? I don't mean to offend you; I know you work in the church and all. But if the Holy Spirit, like the wind, blows wherever it wants and can use all kinds of people, why have church at all?

I actually think that's a great question. In fact, I wish more Christians would ask it.

Really?

Absolutely. If more Christians had a clearer idea of what church is for, I think they'd get a lot more out of it.

Interesting. Okay, then, what *is* the church for?

The church does all kinds of things, but I think most of them can be divided into two broad categories.

Wow, that's pretty simple. Go ahead.

The first has to do with the question you asked earlier. After we talked about how it's okay to have questions and doubts, you asked how we avoid getting stuck in them. How, that is, does faith help us keep our footing amid all the tremors of life?

Right. I remember, but I'm not completely sure I understand how the church does that.

The church, by proclaiming the gospel, helps to create faith in us—faith either to believe in the first place, or to help us continue believing over our lifetime.

What do you mean by "create faith"? I'm not sure I've ever thought about faith as being something you can create.

That's another good question. I don't mean "create" in a mechanical sense. Like, read one chapter of the Bible, pray twice, add water, and stir.

Thank goodness!

Instead, I mean "create" in the sense of "nurture" or "support." Maybe it will help to think back to our discussion of promises.

You mean when you explained how you prefer talking about promises to plans? About how promises actually *do* something to you?

Right. We said two things about promises that might be helpful again. First, promises are always made to specific people. They're very relational in that sense—from one person or group to another. Second, promises are always about the future, about something that hasn't yet happened, and so they create for the person hearing the promise an expectation about the future.

So promises take faith. You have to believe in the future that is being promised.

Definitely. If I tell my kids that I'll be home early from work to take them to a movie and they believe me, they'll get ready; but if they don't believe, they won't. The promise will have failed to create an expectation about the future. So you definitely have to have faith in a promise in order for it to do its job. In the same way, you could say that promises not only depend on faith; they also create it. That is, they give you something to believe and invite you to do so.

And this is what the church does when it tells the story of Jesus.

And especially as it tells why the story of Jesus *matters*.

I'm not sure what you mean.

When we tell the story of Jesus, we're very interested in understanding how this story is *for us*, how it actually involves us. And so the church tells the story of Jesus so that it's not just a historical account of someone who lived long ago, but instead is a story about how God is still involved in our lives, still cares, and is still committed to being in relationship with us. When the story is told that way— about both a person who lived a long time ago *and* what difference that makes to us today—then we might actually *experience* God coming to love, bless, and save all of us and the world.

So it's not just the story of Jesus in general—you know, telling the story for the sake of a good story—but why I should care about that story and what kind of difference that story makes in my life?

Right. We call that—the reason the story of Jesus matters—the *gospel*. That word comes from another word in the Greek language of the New Testament that means "good news." It's "news" in that it tells us about something that happened. But it's "good" because it affects us. It's news that we can't be indifferent to because it affects us.

So if I hear about someone winning the lottery, for instance, that's news. But when I hear that it's *my mom* winning the lottery, that's good news!

Exactly. It makes a big difference when news is personal, when it affects you. And that's essentially what the gospel is—the news of what God has done and is still doing for us and all the world in Jesus. So it's news that involves and *affects* us.

But it sounds like you're also saying that gospel is a promise. It takes faith, because it's not something we can prove.

Yes, the gospel is very much a promise, which means it creates an expectation about the future.

But isn't it also about the past, about Jesus' life, death, and resurrection, all of which happened two thousand years ago?

That's a very good point. The promise is rooted in the past, which means we have to believe something about the past. We believe that there was a guy named Jesus, and that he died and God raised him from the dead. But the promise orients us to the future. *Because* of the cross and resurrection, we believe God *will* always be with us, that God *will* always be for us, that God *will* bring us from death to new life.

I guess, when you think about it, that's how all promises work.

What do you mean?

Well, promises may be about the future, but they're rooted in the past in some sense. I mean, I believe a promise because I've known the person making it, and I trust it because he or she has been trustworthy before. So because of what someone has done in the past, I believe they will keep their promise in the future. In your example, for instance, if you have kept your promises to your kids in the past, they're more likely to believe this one.

That's a great point.

So the church's job is to offer or announce the promise of the gospel, and that helps create or nurture faith?

Yup.

I'm guessing the Sunday sermon is how that's done.

Ideally, that's exactly what you hear in the sermon—the story of the Bible told in a way that makes sense, matters, connects to your life, shows you how much God loves you, and invites you to participate in the kingdom Jesus announced.

I think I'd enjoy a sermon like that. I haven't listened to all that many sermons in recent years, but it seems like most of them are more about telling me what I should do to be a good Christian, if I'm at my sister's church. Or how I need to help other people, if I'm at a church more like we went to when I was a kid. There's nothing wrong with that, I guess, but they haven't exactly "made promises that create faith and orient me to the future."

I know it's probably tempting to use the sermon to tell people what they should be doing, hoping that helps us get more out of life. But I actually think there are enough people already doing that—parents, teachers, coworkers, friends, all kinds of people with good advice. But there aren't a whole lot of people who will tell you that you are inherently worthy of love and respect, that God has blessed you to be a blessing, that God loves you enough to send Jesus to demonstrate that love in word and deed, that God has a role for you to play in blessing our world.

That's true. Most of things I hear—whether on television or the news or at work—is that life is pretty much about proving yourself, about earning your way, about looking out for number one, about buying stuff that will make you happy. I can't think of anyone, except maybe my family—and then on a good day!—who regularly tells me that I'm okay just as I am. And I don't mean "okay" in the sense that I don't have problems or can't improve; I'm keenly aware of my deficiencies. I mean "okay" in the sense that I'm worth it, that I have value, that I'm acceptable. You know what I mean?

I do. And I think that's what the sermon—and really all of church—is about, and why we have church each week and not just once a month or something.

I'm not sure I'm following the part about weekly church.

Well, I suspect that some people think you should go to church to learn how to be a better person, like we were saying. And some people think you should go to church to make God happy. But I think we go to church because it's hard to believe the promise of the gospel for more than about seven days in a row. I mean, think about it: the gospel promises not only that there is a God who created all the universe and still keeps it going, but that this God not only knows about you and me but also cares, really cares deeply and passionately about our ups and downs, about our hopes, fears, and dreams, about our successes and failures and all the rest.

It sounds almost too good to be true.

Exactly, which is why it's hard to believe for more than about seven days in a row. So while you might hear this good news on Sunday, by Friday afternoon . . .

Or, depending on your week, Monday morning!

. . . or by Monday morning, it's just plain hard to believe. And so you go to church to hear this promise broken wide open for you to hear and believe again.

I think if the sermons were like that each week, I might just go.

And it's not just the sermons. The hymns, or songs, that are sung, the biblical readings, the prayers, and especially the sacraments that are celebrated—all these things help express the promises of God, and even make them three-dimensional.

I'm not sure I know what you mean by "sacraments." Baptism is one of them, right?

Yes. Baptism and communion, which is also called the Lord's Supper. These are the two sacraments most Protestant churches celebrate. Roman Catholic and Eastern Orthodox churches have several others. "Sacrament" is connected to our word *sacred*, something that is special, set apart, something that helps us to encounter God in ordinary life.

Can you explain that a little more?

Sure. Augustine called them "visible signs of an invisible reality." Martin Luther described the sacraments as "a promise of God connected to an earthly element." So in baptism you have God's promise to love and forgive us connected to water. Baptism is, for lack of a better term, an "entrance" sacrament. It's the sign and rite by which we are brought into the Christian family publicly. Communion, the promise that God is always with us and for us, always forgiving us and restoring us to relationship with God, is connected to bread and wine. It's essentially an "on the way" or "in the meantime" sacrament. It helps to confirm us in our faith and remind us of our participation in the new community God has formed around Jesus.

There's a lot more we can say, but that might be enough for now.

That's helpful. Thanks.

Sure. And in addition to the sermon, sacraments, and worship, there's also the community of faith itself.

What do you mean?

That one of the ways the Holy Spirit works is through giving us other people to encourage our faith, even at times to believe for us.

I'm not sure I'm following.

Sometimes, when we find faith too hard—like you were describing earlier—it can help to know that you're not alone, that it's not all up to you. Remember, the church is much more than a place or a building; the church is a people, a community.

That's true, but I'm still not sure how other people can believe for us. Isn't faith something we need to do for ourselves?

Some years ago at the school where I teach, an older faculty member lost his wife to illness. It not only broke his heart but also took away his faith. He went to the president and said he felt he should resign. He was so brokenhearted he wasn't sure he believed in God anymore, and if he didn't believe in God, he didn't think he should teach at a seminary. The president gave him a hug and told him that during this time of great sadness and doubt, the rest of the community would believe for him. In the meantime, he could start teaching again whenever he was ready. In time, he did come to believe again.

The community held on to him during that time, "loaning" him their faith, in a sense. Believing for him until he felt he could believe for himself again. Does that make sense?

It does. Some time ago, not too long after my friend's accident, I asked her how she could keep believing in a good God in the midst of all her suffering. She said she didn't always believe, but she knew other people believed, and knowing that helped. I didn't understand what she meant at the time, but I have a better sense now. I think you're right; it helps a lot to know that you're not alone.

I think so, too. As we've seen from the beginning, God gave us each other to be partners in this adventure we call life, and that's true of our life in the church, too.

Okay, so one of the reasons the church exists is to share the gospel—by preaching, worship, the sacraments, and our life together—in order to help us believe. That makes more sense now. You said there were two main purposes, though. What's the other one?

To prepare us for the rest of the week and life in this world.

Would you say more about that? I'll be honest; I haven't usually thought about church this way.

What do you mean?

Well, just that the times I have gone to church it's usually because I feel like I ought to, like someone wants me to—someone in my family, usually. Or I go because it's a special occasion, like Christmas Eve or for a wedding, funeral, or baptism, like my friends just had. But to tell you the truth, I haven't gone because it helps make sense of the rest of my life—you know, my work, my family, my friends, my interests. It actually feels like there's this one place— church—and then there's this other place—real life. But the two don't often have that much to do with each other. I feel a little guilty saying that, but it's true.

I don't think you should feel guilty. I've felt that at times, too.

Really?

Really. But at its best, church prepares you to go out into the world, the place where God is waiting for us to join in God's work of blessing and caring for the world.

Wait, say that again.

At its best, church prepares you to go out into the world, because that's where God is already at work and wants us to join in that work.

But I always thought the place to find God was in church. I mean, that's part of the first reason for the church, right—to tell you that you are loved and made to be a blessing to others? Is God really outside waiting for us, too?

I think we do encounter God—or, maybe better, are encountered *by* God—in church. But that's so we can recognize where God is leading us in the world, so we can join in God's work to bless, like in the promise to Abraham, "all the nations."

Is this about doing the acts of love, mercy, and kindness we've already talked about?

Absolutely. And the amazing thing is that you can do this in your everyday roles as a parent or child, a sibling or friend, an employer or employee, a student or volunteer. Basically, anywhere you are, God has work for you.

You're kidding!

No, I'm not.

But what I do seems so incredibly ordinary—my life, my job, my family—there's nothing terribly earth-shattering about it. How can God work through this to bless the world?

Lots of ways, believe me! And it's not just you. Most of us have pretty ordinary lives, but God can do extraordinary things through them. I mean, think about it. Wherever we are—work, home, school, community—we're often with other people. We can encourage them and help them out.

Are you talking about sharing the gospel story with them or asking them if they're a Christian?

Not so much. I think it's wonderful if you have a chance to share your faith in a way that's welcomed by the person you're talking to. But that's not what I was talking about. You can share in God's work to bless the world by being a friend, a help, or an encouragement. You can also help God by being conscientious in your job, voting, paying your taxes and then making sure they're well spent. Being a good neighbor and citizen, helping out people who are less fortunate— that's partnering with God, too. There are really tons of ways we can live out our Christian life right in our own neighborhood.

I see what you mean. But is that really what God is looking for, or what we mean by saying that God invites us to participate in Jesus' kingdom? It just seems, I don't know, a little small.

Let me try another Bible story.

About Jesus, I'm assuming.

Actually, this one is about his cousin.

Jesus had a cousin?

Yeah, his name is John, and he's better known as John the Baptist. Because that's mostly what we see him doing in the New Testament, baptizing people.

I recognize his name, but I didn't know he was Jesus' cousin.

All the Gospels describe him as something of a fire-and-brimstone preacher, living in the wilderness, looking kind of rough, and definitely causing a stir. Luke's Gospel, which is the one that tells us that Jesus' mother and John's were cousins, also gives us the longest version of one of John's sermons, so we'll look there.

Sounds good.

The beginning and end of the sermon in Luke is pretty similar to what's in Matthew and Mark. John announces that the Messiah, the Jewish savior the prophets talked about, is coming. And then he warns the people to get ready. But Luke has a middle part that no one else records. And it's interesting because after announcing that the Messiah is coming, people come up and ask what they should do to get ready:

And the crowds asked him, "What then should we do?" In reply he said to them, "Whoever has two coats must share with anyone who has none; and whoever has food must do likewise." Even tax collectors came to be baptized, and they asked him, "Teacher, what should we do?" He said to them, "Collect no more than the amount prescribed for you." Soldiers also asked him, "And we, what should we do?" He said to them, "Do not extort money from anyone by threats or false accusation, and be satisfied with your wages." (Luke 3:10-14)

That's it? Share. Be fair. Don't bully. This feels more like the stuff of kindergarten than getting ready for the Messiah.

That might be Luke's point. Being faithful to God doesn't have to be heroic. There are opportunities to do God's will, to be God's people, all around us. These opportunities are going to be shaped by our context—the roles we find ourselves in and the needs of the people around us. But make no mistake; there's no shortage of opportunities staring us in the face. Wherever we live, whether in towns, cities, or rural places, and wherever we go, we can live out our faith in God through service to neighbor.

Well, that lines up with what we're saying, but it's still a little surprising.

What's even more surprising are the people John is talking to.

What do you mean?

They are, at best, the riffraff of John's day. They are poor crowds with little to offer, despised tax collectors who profit from the oppression of their fellow Jews, mercenary soldiers known for extorting the vulnerable. If John instructs, rather than condemns, the lowly poor, the corrupt tax collector, and the bare-knuckled mercenary, then who, we might reasonably ask, is excluded? The answer, as it turns out, is no one.

So everyone has a chance to be part of God's new community formed around Jesus? And I guess that includes me.

It does indeed.

Look, I know when we talk about doing God's work or sharing in the kingdom Jesus brings, it sounds pretty dramatic, and sometimes it may turn out to be that way. But often it's the little things that make a difference in our lives—a teacher who hangs in there with you when you're struggling, a friend who comes to see you when you're sick, a child who faithfully cares for her dad when he's got cancer. All it requires is a little bit of faith to see the sacred in the ordinary.

Seeing the sacred in the ordinary. I like that.

That's what it's about. God blesses us and the whole world in creation. God cares for the world by giving the covenant and the law. Jesus affirms God's original blessing in the Incarnation. And God opens up and promises the possibility of restoring relationship through the atonement. Now God invites us into sharing the news of what God is doing and into participating in God's work through the church.

That makes a lot of sense.

I don't want to limit your imagination about what you or any of us can do, either individually or together. In fact, we might be called to do extraordinary things. But I think it starts by recognizing that God is there, in the ordinary, calling us to be faithful where we are, calling us to care for the world and the people God loves so much right around us. If we take that seriously, then there really is no such thing as a small gesture. God can work through anything for the sake of the world.

With God there is no small gesture. I like that, too. But it can be hard to remember, and even harder to see. The world often doesn't look like a place where God is at work.

And that's exactly what church is all about. At its best, church helps to clarify our vision so that we can see God out in the world at work caring for all people and, indeed, the whole creation.

That actually reminds me of something else C. S. Lewis wrote in his Chronicles of Narnia.

You mean like with the atonement again, how Aslan is really Jesus.

Yes, except this time I'm thinking of a scene much further along in the series. You might remember that as the children get older they're not able to come back to Narnia. In the third book, only Lucy and Edmund are still there, and at the end of their adventure, Aslan tells them that this is their last time in Narnia as well. They're upset because they won't see Aslan again, but then Aslan promises that they can find him in their world, too. And Lucy is surprised and even a little confused.

Because she hasn't realized that he's Jesus.

Right. And then Aslan says that the whole reason they were brought to Narnia is so that they would know him well enough so they could recognize him in their own world.

And that's what you are saying happens at church. We come to hear the gospel promise and to be reminded of how much God loves us. And that actually helps us to go back into the world to look for and find God already at work. And when we recognize God caring for the world, we can join in.

Exactly.

Well, once again I'm kind of bowled over that God would trust us with so much. I'm also a little intimidated when I take it seriously. I mean, even on my best days I make a lot of mistakes. I definitely don't live as I think Jesus would have me live.

None of us do. Which, again, helps to explain what church is all about.

What do you mean?

The whole worship service in most congregations has a certain rhythm to it that gets at what you're describing. Many congregations, for instance, begin with an opportunity for confession and absolution.

You mean when we ask for forgiveness?

Right. It's a time to be honest about what went well and what didn't the last week, about the good we did and the bad, about where we succeeded and where we failed, and everything in between.

So at the beginning of the service we have a chance to tell the truth about ourselves, our condition and our need.

You're catching on! And then through the biblical readings and prayers and sermon and all the rest, we get to hear the second truth that God loves and forgives us so that we're reminded both of who we are and of what God has called us to be.

The two truths again.

Right. And at the same time it's something more. Because after being reminded of who we've been called to be, we're also called and commissioned to do God's work in God's world.

Called and commissioned? I like the way that sounds. By commissioning, do you mean like the kind of commission a person might receive in the armed services?

Yes. It's a bit like that. I suppose you could call it "marching orders." But there's another theological word we use for this. It's *vocation*, which comes from a Latin word that actually means, very simply, "calling." So both Jesus and his cousin John are declaring something like this to us: By virtue of being called through our baptism into the church, we're now commissioned to serve God.

And let me take a shot at what this serving looks like.

Go for it.

We are commissioned—called—to keep and share God's promises. I know how much you like the "promises" language.

Right.

And since the promises are about God restoring relationships, we do our part to help restore our relationships with each other and the creation.

Yes. That's it.

It still feels like quite a gamble.

I know what you mean. It's really something, when you think of it, that God would rely on us so much. And it can actually lend a sense of honor and worth to the otherwise ordinary things we do. I think that's part of what Paul is getting at when he calls the church "the body of Christ" (1 Corinthians 12). He means that God has chosen to work through us no matter what part of the body we are. All parts of the body have an important role to play and make the body what it is. What we do—big or small—when done out of faith, really matters.

I have to admit it would be nice to leave church feeling not only that you're a worthwhile person, but also that what you were going to do all week long was worthwhile and really mattered.

I agree. At its best, church reminds us of how much we are loved, reconnects us with the body of Christ, calls and commissions us to be God's partners in the world, and sends us back out again into the world God loves so much. And then, after another week of working, struggling, striving, and compromising . . .

Compromising?

Sure. A compromise is making the best of an imperfect situation. I think Christians are called to do that all the time, to make the best compromises they can in a broken world for the sake of that world.

I'm not sure the members of my sister's church would go for that.

I realize that if you think the Christian life is an ongoing quest to improve or to become holy, then compromising can sound like a bad thing. But I think we need to take seriously that we live in a sinful world, that our options are therefore sometimes limited, and that we don't always know what the best decision is. And yet we're still called to be faithful in all this, which is different than being called to get it right. I mean, if we wait until we know for sure what we should do or can get everything arranged just as we want it, then we'll never get anything done. So I think we're called to go out and do our best, and sometimes that means compromising.

I like that, but I know it can also be pretty hard at times.

That's right. Martin Luther used to call the church the place where "the consolation and conversation of the faithful" take place. Sometimes we console each other when we're down, discouraged, or need to be reminded of God's love and mercy. And sometimes we join in conversation with other Christians to help us think through the decisions and challenges we face as we try to live out our callings in God's world.

I like that, too, having a place to go where we can really think about what our lives are about and find support to go out and live them.

And after another week of living our lives, of doing our best as imperfect people in an imperfect world, we return to church so that we can be reminded of God's mercy and then called, commissioned, and sent back out one more time.

It feels a little cyclical.

I think it is. Not cyclical as in pointless, though, but cyclical as in rhythmic, like breathing. In fact, I think of this coming to church and going back out to the world again as the respiratory system of the body of Christ. The Holy Spirit breathes us in to be called and commissioned, and breathes us back out into the world to make a difference. Breathed in, breathed out.

I like that image.

I do, too. It helps capture a sense of how life in the church might be and lends a certain kind of logic to the relationship between what God is doing *in* the church and what God is doing *through* the church—us!—out in the world.

I really do like that, and thinking of it as rhythmic rather than simply repetitious helps. But does it ever end? I mean, does it ever come to a close? Is the work ever finished?

Say more.

It seems like Christians also expect Jesus to return again someday, right?

Yes. And that's in the Bible, too.

I'm not sure what that means or how I should feel about it. I guess I'm asking whether there's an end to the biblical story we're talking about.

Sounds like that's what we should talk about next.

Insights and Questions

Church every Sunday is of utmost importance because we need to hear the gospel, be reminded of our sins & be forgiven through Holy Communion and then be reminded what our purpose in life is to LOVE God & one another & To Do Good!

The church is a community of believers that offer support through tough times that we face in life.

CHAPTER 8

The End of All Things
Eschatology

So we've come to the end?

> Well, I don't know if we're *at* the end, but it seems like a good time to talk *about* the end.

And just to be clear, when we say "the end," we're really talking about *the end*, as in the end of the world, the end of history, the end of all things.

> Yes, although I think I'd add, "as we know it."

Like the R.E.M. song—"It's the end of the world as we know it."

> Something like that.

Of course, the next part of the refrain goes, "And I feel fine."

> That's actually not too far from a biblical view of the end.

Really? We should feel *fine* when approaching the end of the world?

> What I'm really thinking of is coming to the end of all things with a sense of confidence, hope, and trust. But I suppose "and I feel fine" isn't too bad a summary. That's where the "as we know it" comes in. Part of the biblical promise is that the end of the world as we know it isn't the complete end, that there's a new beginning after the end.

Whoa. That's a lot to take in at once. Maybe we could back up a bit and start with a more basic question. You mentioned the biblical promise about the end, and I'm curious about how much the Bible says about all this. I mean, does the Bible describe in detail what's going to happen? My sister has read these books about the end of the world, and according to her the authors seem pretty confident that they know what's going to happen.

The Left Behind series?

I think that's it. Honestly, I haven't paid too much attention. When she talks about this stuff, it makes me a little uncomfortable.

In what way?

Well, she seems so confident. Actually, not just confident, but certain. Like there's no doubt. I guess, when I think about it, it's kind of like your issue with talking about God's "plan." It feels like it's all planned out, that things have already been set in motion. What was the term you used to describe that feeling that everything is just chugging on ahead according to God's ultimate plan and we're just riding along?

"Mechanical"?

Right. That's how it feels. Except we're not just going along for the ride. It sounds like we need to make a decision, to "get right with God," as my sister sometimes says, so that we know whether we'll be in heaven or hell.

I can understand how that would make you uncomfortable. It makes a lot of people uncomfortable, including a lot of Christians. Given all we've talked about so far, though, why do you think this way of thinking about the end of the world is appealing, not only to your sister but to a whole lot of people?

That's a good question. I think it might go back to the issue of original insecurity we talked about. I mean, if there's one thing that's going to send your personal anxiety scale through the roof, it's probably thoughts about the world coming to an end. So, feeling like you know what's going to happen and that you get to be on the "winning team" probably really, really helps you feel less anxious, and maybe downright in control.

I think you're probably right.

When you think about it, wanting to know how the world is going to end feels a whole lot like wanting to eat from the tree of the knowledge of good and evil.

That's an interesting way to put it. Because the curious thing is that the more you feel you can read the Bible to predict the future, the less you actually have to trust in your relationship with the God of the Bible. You know what's going to happen, so where does faith come in?

I guess your faith is that the Bible predicts the future accurately and that you've crossed all your celestial t's and dotted your heavenly i's.

Right, which shifts attention from the living and active God, who is never something we can control, to your particular reading of the Bible.

But what does the Bible actually say about all this? Are there predictions about how it's all going to happen? My sister makes it sound like it's all pretty clear, and if that's true, then maybe it makes sense to read it that way. The things she says about these predictions can be pretty convincing.

A number of places in the Bible do talk about the end of the world. I'm not sure I'd call it a dominant theme in Scripture—the way, say, covenant or forgiveness is—but it's still important. And in the end—no pun intended!—that's a good thing.

Really, in what way?

As we've talked about before, the Bible is a story that begins in the very beginning and ends at the very end. Which, among other things, means that it invites us to find ourselves in it, to make this story our own. So by including the end of the world as part of its story, the Bible can help to create a sense of confidence about where we're heading.

Confidence and certainty don't sound exactly the same.

Good point. They're not. And I think it's important for me to be clear right up front that I think the Bible makes *promises* about the end rather than offers a *blueprint* to the end. Which means we may not know exactly *how* everything is going to work out, but we still have a promise that, in the end, it *will* work out. That it will come to a *good* end.

209

And what exactly constitutes "a good end"?

Great question. In general, I think it's safe to say that a good end is where God has kept God's promises, where the broken relationships between God and us and between each other have been restored, and where God's intentions for creation have been realized.

Could you be a little more specific?

I can try. But it's more challenging than it may appear, as even the Bible sticks with promise language. So, for example, what we have in the Bible are promises that, in due time, God will "be all in all" (1 Corinthians 15:28), that God will "wipe every tear from their eyes" and "death and mourning will be no more" (Revelation 21:4), and that God will "do a new thing," actually making "all things new" (Isaiah 43:19; Revelation 21:5). These promises are concrete—in the sense that they promise an end to the hardships of this life and a restored and re-created life and creation. But they are also fairly broad. Meaning the Bible doesn't tell us everything about what it will be like. Which both invites and puts limits on our imagination.

What do you mean?

When you hear promises like this, it's hard not to fill them in with your imagination. I think that's part of how promises work: they invite you to imagine what the "kept promise" will look like. At the same time, there's only so much we can say about this promised future, so we probably shouldn't be overconfident that it will turn out the way we've imagined.

So this kind of promise invites both imagination and *humility*.

That's a nice way of putting it.

Well, I suppose I shouldn't be surprised by your emphasis on promises and the need to distinguish between a promise and a plan. That's been important throughout our conversations on sin, incarnation, atonement—actually just about everything!

And it will be really important as we talk about eschatology, too.

I assume you'll say a little more about what in the world *eschatology* means?

No problem. It probably sounds like the most complicated of all the theological terms we've talked about, or probably the least familiar. But it's actually pretty simple. You already know what anything with *ology* at the end means.

Sure, from *logos*, or "words"—so it means "words about" or "the study of."

Right. And *eschatos* is a Greek word that means "the last" as in "last things," "final," or "end."

So *eschatology* means "the study of the last things." You're right; that was easy.

So with that in mind, maybe it would help to look at some of the particular parts of the biblical story that talk about "the final things" and see if they really do describe things as the Left Behind series and other such books do, or whether they point in another direction.

I think that's a good idea.

Okay, so we'll start by talking about a kind of literature called "apocalyptic," which I know is another odd word, but one you might have heard used before.

Like in *Apocalypse Now* or Mel Gibson's *Apocalypto*? I think I've heard it used when people talk about nuclear holocaust or other frightening end-of-the-world scenarios. Judging from all this, I assume it refers to a kind of scary discussion of "last things."

I think that's the way most of us have experienced the word. Surprisingly, it actually just means "revelation" or a "lifting of a veil," where someone is given a vision of the future usually, like you just said, leading to the end of the world.

But you said it's a kind of literature? What did you mean by that?

Writings are often grouped with other writings that share similar literary conventions and patterns. While there may be all kinds of different romance novels, for instance, on a whole they are a different kind of literature than historical biographies, just as science fiction is different from journalism. When we read, we often unconsciously place what we're reading into one of these literary categories. And that decision shapes how we read it. For this reason, when people confuse established categories, that can really interfere with how they read and understand something.

Like when people in the thirties thought Orson Welles's radio adaptation of *The War of the Worlds* was an actual news bulletin and panicked because they thought Martians really were invading New Jersey.

Exactly. So just as there is prophetic literature and wisdom literature, there is also apocalyptic literature, and it helps to keep them straight.

Wait a minute—aren't prophecies also about the future? So what's the difference between prophetic literature and apocalyptic literature?

That's an important question. These two are often confused with each other. Prophets tend to speak to distinct historical situations and address their communities with specific warnings about the consequences of their present ethical and religious practices. For instance, two regular themes of the prophets of Israel are devotion to God and proper treatment of the poor and vulnerable.

Sounds like the two relationships God is always concerned with. And if I remember correctly, the prophets usually thought about them together. That is, right relationship with God implies right relationship with each other.

That's right. And the prophets always addressed their message to specific people with specific concerns. So when the prophets talked about the future, it was usually in terms of very immediate warnings to the people about the consequences of their actions. Even when they used powerful symbols, those symbols usually referred to concrete situations that the hearers would have understood.

So most of what we call "prophecy" was less about the future than the present.

Right, or at least the immediate future. The big exception, of course, were the times when the prophets occasionally looked ahead to God's ultimate redemption, when they made promises about a distant time in the future. But those really were promises, not predictions about a course of action or a blueprint of history.

So what's different about apocalyptic literature?

Whole books have been written on this topic, of course, but we can probably touch briefly on a couple of important features of apocalyptic literature that can help us avoid making the kind of category mistake that plagued Orson Welles's radio audience.

I'm all ears.

First, apocalyptic literature comes out of a dualistic worldview.

A what?

Dualism is a view of the world where there are always two layers of reality, one that is historical and concrete and which we experience firsthand, and a second that is spiritual, eternal, and not readily apparent. These two layers are tied to each other, even reflect each other, but the spiritual is the more important one. So what happens in the spiritual realm is lived out, or experienced, in the historical realm.

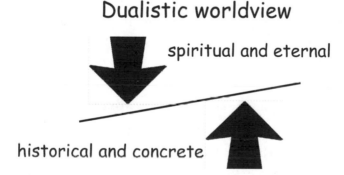

Dualistic worldview

spiritual and eternal

historical and concrete

Which means that what I'm experiencing in my world is a result of something that's happening in another, spiritual world that I can't perceive?

Exactly. Which is what makes apocalyptic literature so appealing—it literally tears aside the veil that separates the historical and the spiritual so that you can make sense of your life by fitting it into a larger, cosmic picture.

From what I gather about Revelation from what my sister says, it seems like that larger, cosmic picture is fairly violent.

That's a second feature of dualistic, apocalyptic literature. It usually imagines that human history involves a cosmic battle between the forces of good and evil and, in particular, between God and God's enemies. More often than not, apocalyptic literature places the current problems and circumstances of its readers into this larger cosmic story of the struggle and eventual triumph of God over all the forces of evil.

So it sounds like, in a way, apocalyptic literature is also focused on the present. Because the visions about the future are intended to make sense of the present—to put it in a bigger picture—not just predict the future.

That's a key observation.

Which means that knowing the actual circumstances of the original audience is probably pretty important.

It might be more accurate to say that apocalyptic literature deals with problems in the present by projecting them into the future. It's not as here-and-now oriented as prophetic literature. At the same time, you're absolutely right: the story about the future is told to make the present hardships more tolerable. So, understanding the historical circumstances behind the apocalyptic writing is very helpful. In the case of Revelation, for instance, the Christians that John was writing to . . .

So—sorry to interrupt. Is this the same John who wrote the Gospel?

For a long time Christians assumed he was. But the author of Revelation, who names himself "John," never claims to have seen Jesus in the flesh and even refers to the twelve apostles but doesn't include himself among him. John was a pretty common name then, as it is now, so the author is probably another early Christian named John. Sometimes he's called John the Seer.

Okay, thanks. And you were about to mention something about the original audience?

Yes. It seems likely that the Christians John addressed were suffering persecution from the Romans, and John was writing to encourage them to keep the faith. In Revelation, Rome is the beast, the new Babylon—because the Romans destroyed the second temple, just as the Babylonians had destroyed the first temple—and they are now beginning to persecute Christians. But John says that this empire won't last forever; that if you look into the spiritual realm, you get a glimpse of the larger picture and, most importantly, of the victory to come.

When you describe it this way, it seems pretty straightforward. But I have to say I often find the conversations my sister tries to have with me about all this pretty confusing. For instance, there are all these really weird symbols and images. I've heard her talk not only about the beast—which you're saying is Rome—but also about four horsemen, a lamb, throne, sealed scrolls, and other stuff that I have a hard time keeping straight.

Which is a third aspect about apocalyptic literature worth considering. Apocalyptic literature often is very symbolic. In part, that's because the writers are trying to describe a spiritual and cosmic realm, and ordinary language just doesn't seem to be adequate for that. So they use vivid images and symbols to help bridge the gap between our ordinary experience and the extraordinary and cosmic reality the writer is trying to convey.

That's helpful. I can see how hard it would be to describe the cosmic world apart from vivid images.

The heavy symbolism might stem from the fact that apocalyptic literature is often written to people suffering persecution or oppression.

Which is why the message that their struggles are part of a larger story is so appealing in the first place.

Right. And if they're currently suffering persecution, then it might not be safe to write plainly.

So if you've got Romans checking up on you, maybe it's safer to talk about Babylon or a beast than Rome.

Exactly. Using an elaborate system of symbols lets you encode a pretty subversive message: "Resist the Empire."

That makes a lot of sense and is pretty interesting to think about. But it also gets a little confusing.

Absolutely. Images and symbols always open themselves up to multiple interpretations. On the one hand, that makes apocalyptic literature more difficult to read and can result in a lot of strange interpretations.

I'll say!

On the other hand, though, there's also something useful about the ambiguity or flexibility of symbols.

Really?

Yeah. I mean, it's very important to try to hear apocalyptic literature as the original audience would have heard it so that you don't interpret it totally out of context. At the same time, however, if it only deals with the issues and circumstances of that particular audience, then there's not much incentive to keep reading it. So whether the writers were trying to be "deliberately ambiguous" or whether that's just a by-product of all the symbols and imagery, we keep reading Revelation today precisely because its symbols and imagery can speak to more than one set of circumstances.

But can't that be dangerous?

Definitely, and there are plenty of examples of poor interpretations out there. But the same imagery that might preoccupy the people writing and reading the Left Behind series has also inspired some of the most famous and meaningful Christian art and music.

Really?

Sure. Have you ever heard of "Battle Hymn of the Republic" or Handel's "Hallelujah Chorus"?

Of course.

Both were inspired by different sections of Revelation.

I never knew that.

In each case, the composer was inspired by the vivid language and imagery of the book to write a song that spoke that same kind of confidence and courage into our own lives.

They didn't take it as a blueprint of the future.

Not at all, but they saw enough parallels between what John was describing and their own circumstances that they could set the promises of Revelation to song in a way that inspired countless others. So it's important to keep in mind the historical circumstances of apocalyptic literature so that we don't misread it badly—as so many have done over the years with Revelation. On the other hand, it's also important to remember that the God John witnesses to is the same God who inspired the rest of the Bible and seeks to draw *us* into relationship—in this case by making promises about the ultimate hopefulness of the future.

It sounds like we're back to promises. Is that the best way to read Revelation, as a book making promises?

I think so. And those promises have both a concrete historical character—to the Christians suffering persecution in Rome—and a more general character that can speak to us today.

Is this true of all apocalyptic literature? And by the way, how many books in the Bible are apocalyptic?

Apocalyptic literature isn't all the same any more than all romance novels are the same. But they do share the characteristics we've been talking about. So we can read them with an eye to our circumstances as well as to those of the original audience. In the Christian Bible there are two main books that are pretty thoroughly apocalyptic in character: Revelation in the New Testament and the second half of Daniel in the Old Testament. But there are other books, including Isaiah, some letters of Paul, and most of the Gospels, that have brief apocalyptic scenes or references.

The Gospels are apocalyptic?

No, they aren't apocalyptic as a whole, but they do have brief apocalyptic scenes. This can get a little confusing, I know, but it will help to keep in mind that we're talking about "apocalyptic" first and foremost as a literary type that reflects a distinct, dualistic view of the world.

Okay.

With that in mind, then we can talk about how both Paul and the authors of the Gospels definitely operated from the conviction that, in Jesus, God has entered decisively into human events to defeat sin and death and restore our broken relationships with God and each other.

This is the "kingdom of God" stuff we talked about, the kingdom that Jesus preaches.

Right. So in this sense both Paul and the Gospel writers believe that God really has gotten into the game in a new way, and that a new era has started. But that's not the same as writing in an apocalyptic style or working from a dualistic view of the world.

But you said there are parts of the Gospels and Paul and some other books that are apocalyptic.

Yes, there are particular scenes or passages. They may have been written to help answer the question of why Jesus had not yet returned when so many early believers thought he would be coming back soon. And they may have also been written to comfort early Christian communities that were experiencing persecution.

The early Christians thought that Jesus was returning right away?

Early on, many of the first Christians did, including Paul. They thought that the kingdom Jesus started would be completed during their lifetime. But when it became apparent that it wouldn't, the early Christians looked ahead in certain passages to talk about when Jesus would come again.

On the whole, it sounds like the primary reason for writing apocalyptic stuff—whether as a whole book or a part of the book—was to help people who were struggling with faith because of the immediate hardships they faced. They needed promises to continue to believe that God was behind everything and would bring them through.

I think that's right. In the case of the Gospels, one of the ways the authors responded to the struggle of believers waiting for Jesus was to place it into a larger picture of how God was working through history. This gave their communities hope that their story was a part of this larger story, a story with a promised good ending.

That's helpful, but I still have to say that I'm a little uncomfortable with how violent apocalyptic writing seems to be. You can see why moviemakers would choose a word like *apocalyptic* to describe their most violent films.

I think you should be uncomfortable. In fact, I think we should all be uncomfortable. What may have been a perfectly reasonable solution to the problem of persecution two thousand years ago is not necessarily reasonable today.

But it seems like if we want the confidence and courage that apocalyptic literature offers, don't we also have to accept some of the dualism and violence as well?

No, I don't think we do. Eschatology—a concern with the end of the story, so to speak—is a larger category than apocalyptic, which was only one way of talking about the end. And while some sections of the New Testament are apocalyptic, most of it is definitely not.

So do we just ignore the apocalyptic writings?

Some Christians would love for us to do that, and I can understand why. All the violence and bloodshed feel so much *not* like the Jesus we read about in the Gospels. But I don't think ignoring or downplaying the apocalyptic elements is an option for two reasons. First, I don't want to surrender all this material to the apocalyptic Christians of our own age. If we simply sit back and refuse to deal with Revelation and the rest, then the folks who are misinterpreting it so badly win the day by default. There's too much at stake to sit by and let that happen.

I, for one, wouldn't mind having something to say back to my sister. I don't mean that I have to win any arguments. I'd just like to be able to offer another voice in the conversation.

Exactly. A second, and perhaps more important, reason we can't ignore the apocalyptic literature in the Bible is that there's little doubt that most early Christians had a strong sense that God had entered into human affairs to set things right. And some of them used an apocalyptic frame of reference to explain their convictions. So even if we find it uncomfortable, I think it's important that we take apocalyptic passages seriously and allow them to inform our larger discussion about eschatology and the question of how God brings things to a good end.

And how do we do that?

For starters, we can recognize that the early church tried to answer questions about Jesus' delayed return and about their own persecution and suffering in a variety of ways. Apocalyptic literature was just one of them.

What were some of the others?

Sometimes, when they thought Jesus was returning soon, they encouraged believers to wait expectantly. A good example of that is 1 Thessalonians 5. At other times, when they realized the church would be here for a much longer time, they suggested ways to organize the emerging church, as in 1 Timothy 3. And there were all kinds of options in between. In short, there was no single way to think about how God was keeping God's promises during the years the New Testament was being written. So it's not surprising that we find a number of approaches, sometimes reflected in a single book.

This sounds pretty complicated. Where do we go from here?

As we've said, once the early Christians realized that Jesus was not coming back as immediately as they first thought, they proposed all kinds of ways to think about how God would keep God's promises. And that's reflected in the diversity of approaches in the New Testament. Ever since, the church has tried to draw these different proposals into some kind of meaningful order.

And is that what eschatology is, then—reflection on all the talk about "last things" found in the Bible?

Yes, that's just what it is.

Are there any common threads or patterns?

Yes. While this may oversimplify things just a little, we can divide most ways of dealing with the diversity of material relating to the end in the Bible—in both the Old and New Testaments—into two broad categories.

Wait. We've been focusing mainly on the New Testament. There's also eschatology in the Old Testament?

Absolutely. As we mentioned, the second half of Daniel is apocalyptic. At points many of the prophets raise their gaze from their immediate concerns and context and look forward to God's eventual "new thing" and "new day," some of which also involves the end of time.

Okay, so there's lots of diversity in the ways "the end" is talked about, not only in the New Testament but also throughout the Bible. But if we really can boil this down a little, that would help a lot.

I think we can, as long as we keep in mind that these categories are most useful for organizing our own thoughts about the "last things." We can't expect any of the biblical books to fit neatly into any one category without flattening some of the diversity represented there.

Got it. So what's the first point of view?

The first view is often called a "future eschatology," because it reads all of the references to Jesus' return and God's anticipated intervention into the world as referring to a literal, concrete future time.

Future Eschatology

PAST	PRESENT	FUTURE
God intervenes		Jesus returns

Well, that seems pretty straightforward. And it sounds like the apocalyptic literature we were talking about.

> You're right. Apocalyptic literature falls generally into this category. Although, even with apocalyptic literature, it can be difficult to know how far into the future the early Christians imagined God's action would be.

What do you mean?

> Take Revelation as an example. It's difficult to know if the early Christian readers of that book thought that the visions of God's triumph that John revealed were in the immediate or distant future. There's a certain urgency to John's writing, so it might be that the Christians who first read Revelation expected John's visions to be fulfilled soon. It's only later Christians who projected them into the more distant future.

That might explain why Revelation seems so intriguing to some Christians today. After two thousand years, the future that once seemed distant might now feel like it's just around the corner, especially if they read the urgency of John's writing as relating to our time instead of to his time.

> I think you're right. Which is why it's so important to read the books of the Bible in light of their historical context.

So what's the purpose of a future eschatology? Is it to make sense of why Jesus hasn't come back yet, or to comfort Christians who are suffering?

> I think the goal is to give comfort to believers by placing their current struggle in a larger framework and to encourage them to stay faithful in the meantime.

Interesting. And the other point of view?

> The other point of view interprets most of what Scripture says about the "last things" as having already started, or as having been fulfilled with the coming of Jesus. This is called a "realized eschatology," meaning that the things promised have already started or even have already been realized in Jesus.

Realized Eschatology

PAST	PRESENT	FUTURE

God intervened
in Jesus

Can you say a little more about this one?

Sure. The important point is to notice that a central element in Jesus' preaching in Matthew, Mark, and Luke is that "the kingdom of God has drawn near" or "is close at hand." A realized eschatology thinks that Jesus wasn't predicting something off in the future but, in fact, was referring to his own preaching and teaching and, specifically, his crucifixion and resurrection. That is, God's kingdom comes in Jesus' death and resurrection, and so all the stuff that sounds like it's about the future is really fulfilled in the cross and resurrection. For instance, in Mark's Gospel, right after a short apocalyptic section about the end time, Jesus says the following:

> "But about that day or hour no one knows, neither the angels in heaven, nor the Son, but only the Father. Beware, keep alert; for you do not know when the time will come. It is like a man going on a journey, when he leaves home and puts his slaves in charge, each with his work, and commands the doorkeeper to be on the watch. Therefore, keep awake—for you do not know when the master of the house will come, in the evening, or at midnight, or at cockcrow, or at dawn, or else he may find you asleep when he comes suddenly. And what I say to you I say to all: Keep awake." (Mark 13:32-37)

I don't know—that sounds pretty future-oriented to me, and pretty good advice if you think the world will end soon.

Right, except what's interesting is that the four times of day that Jesus mentions that the master of the house might come—evening, midnight, cockcrow, or dawn—correspond with Mark's description of events that are about to happen and lead to Jesus' passion. So the scenes he shares over the next two chapters are: 1) Passover and garden—evening; 2) arrest and trial—midnight; 3) Peter's denial—cockcrow; and 4) trial before Pontius Pilate—dawn.

So are you saying that Mark is saying that the "hour" that no one knows about is really the cross?

That's one way to read it from the point of view of a realized eschatology. And in that case, then all that came just before—including the clear apocalyptic language—also refers not to some future event but to the cross. So that eschatology isn't about something "out there" that we are waiting for, but instead is saying that it all got started with Jesus' life, ministry, death, and resurrection. We are already living in a new age.

Interesting. It seems like that kind of view would really change your focus. Instead of looking out into the future for God's coming work, you'd be more likely to look around you.

That's a very important observation. Champions of a realized eschatology would say that one of the major problems of a future eschatology is precisely that it doesn't have any meaningful ethical implications. If God is going to bring history to a close at an appointed time in the future, then there's not much Christians need to do except watch, pray, and stay faithful.

So why bother worrying about global warming or nuclear war if it's all part of God's plan?

Right.

It sounds like one of the great values of a realized eschatology is that it emphasizes ethical responsibility in the here and now.

Yes. God has already done what God came to do, and we are invited to participate actively in the new age God inaugurated. Not only that, but we have an example of what that looks like in Jesus, who not only ushered in God's kingdom but also showed us in word and deed what life in the new kingdom looks like.

Again, very interesting. What do you think?

Can you guess? I'll give you a clue: In this case past performance is a pretty good indicator of future performance.

Given that, I'm guessing that you like something about both points of view, but you don't want to be limited to any single theory or plan.

Right on the money! Actually, I have the hardest time with the more extreme versions of a future eschatology that anticipate or even promote the violent destruction of people and the earth. That is not really in line with the witness of the Bible. Even in Revelation, or maybe I should say especially in Revelation given how regularly it is misused, there is a promise of renewal that is far more than simply starting over. And as for the "Left Behind" sense that Christians should seek to escape the problems of this world and leave everyone else behind, there's nothing like that in the Bible. In Revelation, the end is signaled when God comes to dwell with us, not when we escape to some peaceful heaven.

Although maybe if you're a persecuted community, or at least feel like you're being persecuted, then wanting a violent defeat of your persecutors or the promise that God will take you out of a hostile world makes sense.

That's a very good point. Maybe holding on to an extreme future eschatology says more about you than it does about the Bible.

So you're more in the realized eschatology camp?

I'd say I've got at least one foot planted solidly there because I do think that everything is different after Jesus' death and resurrection.

Especially the resurrection.

Right. At the same time, though, I think there's got to be more to the Bible's promises than God more or less saying, "Well, I've done my part; now it's up to you."

Yeah. I think I see what you mean. We've had two thousand years and not much has changed. So if it's all up to us, we probably can't hold out much hope that things will ever really be different.

Exactly, which is why some measure of a more future-oriented or transcendent sense of God's activity is helpful.

What do you mean by "transcendent"?

That God is at work not only in and through us, but also beyond us. That there are some things we can't achieve on our own; that we still need God to bring things to a good end, one that we maybe can't see or create for ourselves but that we hope for nonetheless.

So God has gotten things started, and we're invited to continue them. But God is the one who will also need to bring them to a close, to a good end.

That's it. Do you remember our description of the Holy Spirit as the one who both helps us to believe and draws us into God's work in the world? Well, Paul at times speaks of the Holy Spirit as God's "down payment," "guarantee," or "first installment" on what is to come.

A tangible down payment that guarantees what's still coming. I like that. Is there a term for this point of view? Maybe a "realized-future eschatology"?

Well, you know how leery I am about theories. They're useful for organizing stuff, but they don't always reflect our experience as honestly as I'd like.

There is a phrase in theology, though, that captures what I think our actual experience is of being invited to participate in God's kingdom while simultaneously waiting for God to bring it to completion.

Yes . . . ?

"Already but not yet."

That's it? No fancy Latin or Greek words?

Nope. I know what you mean; it's not exactly an impressive name, but it does describe the Christian conviction that God's kingdom is *already* among us but *not yet* fully or completely. Or, maybe better, God's decisive action has already happened in Christ and we can both feel and participate in that, but at the same time we don't yet experience the full outcome of that victory.

I think I see. It's kind of like this one aunt I had growing up.

I can't say I'm following you, but I know I'll catch on eventually.

Well, she had this way of always choosing the best birthday gifts for me. It wasn't that they were big or fancy or particularly expensive. Often they were quite the opposite, really quite ordinary. But they always seemed perfectly suited to me, to what age I was, to what I was going through at the time. It was uncanny, but it was like she totally knew me, and so she knew just what little thing would mean a lot to me.

That's really neat. But I'm still not making the connection.

The thing was, she always sent them late. They never, ever came on my birthday. Sometimes it was a day or two late, but usually more like two or three weeks. And one time it came nearly four months late.

That must have been frustrating at times.

A little, but honestly not that much. You see, because I'd already had some experience of her great gifts before, I had reason to believe the next one would be just as cool, so I knew it was worth waiting for.

That's a really interesting analogy. I think that is something like what the already-not-yet experience is like. In our worship service there's a song that talks about the "foretaste of the feast to come." It's kind of like we've had an appetizer, so we know there is great food out there, but we're still waiting for the main course.

"Already, Not Yet"

PAST	PRESENT	FUTURE
Jesus' cross & resurrection		Jesus returns God renews everything

But how do we prevent this viewpoint from making us lazy, just waiting for the end to come? That seems like the weakness of the analogies we just used. There wasn't much I could do except wait for my aunt's gift to arrive.

That's a great question. On the one hand, I don't think there's anything we can do to totally prevent it. I mean, if you don't feel like doing anything for the people around you in need, I probably can't motivate you otherwise. At the same time, if you are at all interested in "realizing" the kingdom in your own life and world, than an "already-not-yet" perspective can be very motivating, perhaps even more so than a realized eschatology.

How so?

Well, I can't compel anyone to take care of our neighbors or the world. But if you believe that God has acted in Jesus—to bring the kingdom of God, or inaugurate a new era, or fashion a new creation, or however you might describe it—and if you look to Jesus to see what that new kingdom looks like—feeding the poor, caring for the sick, comforting those who are discouraged, working for justice and the like— then you're totally free just to throw yourself into that work.

What do you mean?

Well, you can just do it—whatever it is you're trying to do—without worrying about whether you'll change the world or not. I mean, sometimes the problems all around us seem so great there doesn't seem to be much point in trying at all. Like, why ride the bus instead of driving when you see how much pollution there is? Or why bother sending $10 to feed a starving child when so many kids are starving?

I know what you mean. I've felt totally discouraged at times because I couldn't see what difference my paltry little efforts would make.

Right. So the already-not-yet of the gospel says that, since God has promised to take care of the universal problems—like redeeming the world!—then we're free to work on the ones right in front of us.

So if I don't have to take care of the really big problems, I'm free to look after the little ones?

Who knows whether they'll be little or big? I mean, there are definitely all kinds of "little" things you can do, like helping a neighbor, or going to a community forum to advocate for a new playground or low-income housing. But Christians have also worked toward some really huge things, like leading the anti-slavery movement in Great Britain and the United States in the nineteenth century, protesting and helping end apartheid in the twentieth, and leading some of the conservation efforts in the twenty-first.

Those are some pretty amazing examples. It's hard to imagine doing that.

If you think about doing it all by yourself, it is hard to imagine. But as part of the church, both local congregations as well as the larger church, we can do all kinds of things.

That's encouraging to remember.

What I'm really trying to stress is that there's a powerful freedom in the Bible's promise that God will, in time, redeem the world. That promise frees us to give everything we have in our effort to live the kingdom Jesus started and not worry about whether we succeed, because we have Jesus' promise that what he started he will also finish.

And is that what the Bible says, that God will take care of the whole world?

That's where Revelation's language of God creating "a new heaven and a new earth" and of "wiping every tear from their eyes" becomes quite powerful (Revelation 21:1-4). And it's not only Revelation, but also Paul, who—whatever he thought about how soon Jesus would return—wrote that the whole creation "groans" in anticipation of being renewed (Romans 8:19-23).

Which means I don't have to save the whole world, because God will. And that frees me to take care of my corner of it.

Exactly.

That reminds me of the story of the star thrower by the anthropologist Loren Eiseley, though I can't remember where I read it. He tells about a young man walking on the beach one morning who comes upon an older man who's throwing starfish into the sea. He watches for a little while as the guy throws starfish after starfish back into the ocean and then asks him what he's doing. The older guy says that the starfish are stranded, and if they don't get back into the ocean before noon, they'll dry out and die. The young guy looks up

and down, seeing thousands upon thousands of starfish, and asks the older one what difference he can possibly make. The older man picks up one more, hurls it into the ocean, and says, "To the ones I throw back into the sea, it's all the difference in the world."

That's a great story.

Yeah, I haven't thought about it in ages, but it seems like that's totally the point here. We may be called to take care of the whole world, but we're not the ones responsible for redeeming it. God will do that in time, which means that we're free to do what we can, sometimes maybe even making a world of difference right where we are.

I think it not only frees us but also can give us courage to face what look like daunting tasks or insurmountable odds.

How so?

One biblical scholar once described this point of view as something like the time between D-Day, when the Allies stormed the beaches at Normandy on June 6, 1944, and V-E Day, the day victory was won in Europe on May 8, 1945.

I'm not sure I follow.

Well, once the Allies successfully landed at Normandy, there was little doubt about the eventual outcome of the war; they would most certainly prevail. But it turned out there were still ten months of brutal fighting to go. Many soldiers continued to give their strength, their limbs, their lives. Still, knowing they were giving themselves in the cause of victory made all the difference. I mean, it's one thing to sacrifice for a lost cause and another altogether to sacrifice for one that you know is right and will prevail.

So in Jesus' cross, and especially his resurrection, you have the successful landing at Normandy.

Right. Jesus' resurrection signals that God has conquered death. That's the down payment, the foretaste of final victory. It's something we can hold on to even as we wait for our own resurrection and the redemption of the world.

And his coming again at the end of time to create a new heaven and earth and to wipe the tears from every eye is V-E Day.

Exactly. In the meantime, we struggle on, not always seeing the difference what we do makes, but counting on the promise that we're struggling and sacrificing for a winning cause.

That's powerful. And it does seem like it would be encouraging to have a future sense of what God will do, as well as a realized sense of what God has already done and invites us to do. If you don't expect to see everything change because of what you're doing, then you're less likely to get discouraged when everything doesn't change.

Right. So we live between these two decisive acts of God. One is in the past. That's Jesus' cross and resurrection. And one is still to come in the future. That's Christ's coming again and God's promised renewal of all creation. In between, we're free to throw ourselves into life and all that's around us. In this time between, we can imitate the kingdom Jesus initiated, even while we look forward to its fulfillment at the end of time.

Which makes the present a lot more hopeful, and gives us something to do beyond simply waiting around for the end of the world to come.

Exactly. I've seen it play out powerfully in people's individual lives as well. The hope of God's promised future lends some courage to the challenges of the present. I had an aunt who struggled with cancer at the end of her life. As she neared death in the hospital, she would toast her husband during the dinners they shared with the words from the worship service I mentioned a bit ago. She'd say, "Here's to the feast to come."

I think that's something my dad would find helpful, too. Not heaven as an escape, but a sense that when you've done everything you can do, God is still there with you.

That reminds me. I remember seeing a huge ad emblazoned on a semi-trailer of a major car company that read, "Belief in the present comes from faith in the future." I always liked the sound of that, which is probably why I remember it. It seems like that sort of sums up the value of eschatology in relation to the rest of the Christian story.

That's right. I think having some sense of the end of the story—not all the details but how it eventually comes out—helps us hang in there for the hard parts.

Like when I finally was old enough to watch *The Wizard of Oz* all the way through.

You mean your parents wouldn't let you watch when you were little?

No, they'd let me. I don't know if they should have, but they would. The thing is, the first couple of times I saw it, I'd always run out of the room at the scary parts.

Like when the flying monkeys came, I bet.

Or that scene on the road when the witch lights Scarecrow on fire. Those scenes terrified me. Eventually I got old enough to know that no matter how afraid I might be during those scenes, it would turn out okay. It didn't make those parts less scary, but it helped me hang in there.

Yeah, I see what you mean. We might not know the ending of all things in the same detail as we know the end of a movie, but we have a promise that it will, in the end, have a good ending. And that promise makes all the difference.

Which brings us back to the idea of promises again, and just how fragile faith can be sometimes.

Very much so. We can't prove any of this. Not Jesus' future return, not the new heaven and earth, none of it. Not only that, but when you really think about it, we can't prove the earlier part, either.

About Jesus and the resurrection?

Right. After all, we weren't there. Not only that, but all kinds of people who were there didn't believe it. I know a lot of people have tried to prove that the Bible is true, or that Jesus was raised from the dead. And maybe those kinds of arguments are helpful to some, but in the end what we have in the New Testament is a collection of confessions about who Jesus was and is, and about what God was and is up to through him.

Calling them confessions not only makes more sense to me, but also seems to leave more room for belief. As we've said before, if you can prove it, what's to believe? But faith calls for you to get involved, to take part, to take a risk and place your bet on this story rather than some other one.

That's right. Faith, I like to say, is made up of equal measures of *imagination*—the ability to imagine a God of love passionately committed to drawing us and all the world into relationship with God—and *courage*—daring to believe even when there's precious little evidence. That's definitely what the early Christians did. I mean, their confession was absolutely the minority report; most people didn't believe it.

Why do you think the early Christians did believe it? I mean, what tipped them from doubt to faith?

Well, the earliest Christians had some direct experience with Jesus—certainly when he was first alive, but also after the resurrection.

It seems like not all Christians believe that, including some authors of pretty popular books about Jesus. Do you have to believe in Jesus' physical resurrection to be a Christian?

To be honest, I'm not all that interested in deciding who gets to claim being a Christian and who doesn't. I realize that some people have a very hard time imaging a physical, bodily resurrection because it runs contrary to their sense of an ordered, closed, physical universe. And once you introduce the possibility of God raising some people—even one person—from the dead, all that is at risk and you have to start wondering why God doesn't get involved and raise, or at least heal, all kinds of people. So I get why making the resurrection a spiritual thing is appealing to some very intelligent Christian thinkers.

But . . .

But at the same time, I just don't think there's any denying that the earliest Christians really believed in a physical resurrection. Everything points to the fact that they had an experience of the Risen Christ and expected bodily resurrection at the end of time. So I think that no matter how much we might be tempted to psychologize the resurrection and call it the resurrection of their faith, or the new birth of hope, or a vision of the kingdom, or whatever, I just don't think we can get around their confession that the resurrection of Jesus is at the center of the faith. It was for Paul; it was for the Gospel writers; and it remains a central mark of the Christian story today.

Because of the way it shows how God keeps promises?

Right. And God's promise kept in the resurrection—even when taken on faith—anchors our faith that God will keep God's promises about the end as well.

Faith, as we've said before, really is a fragile thing.

It is. And at the same time, it's incredibly strong.

"Able to move mountains," I think someone once said.

But maybe, most of all, faith is an active thing.

Say a little more.

Well, I think faith is restless. It can't quite ever be grounded once and for all. In that sense, it's not quite like knowledge. You can't sit back and evaluate the claims made by faith in the same way you can evaluate claims that depend on verifiable knowledge. That's because faith—to be faith—transcends what we can know on our own and draws us into relationship with the object of our faith itself.

But the hard thing is that knowledge seems so appealing, so much safer.

It always has, even for our great-great-grandparents Adam and Eve. But while knowledge might be safer, it's not nearly as exciting.

What do you mean?

Faith requires that you get in the game. It's one thing to sit back and describe the Christian story or even try to evaluate how well it holds together compared to other stories, and so forth. But that's not really faith. Faith is when you finally believe—or not—and make this story your own. You know?

I think I do. And I think I can . . . make it my own, that is.

That's really encouraging to hear.

It's funny. I think that when I started this conversation I was looking for answers, trying to see whether faith would help me understand what's going on with my dad and with my friend. But I think what I've found isn't so much answers but hope. You know what I mean? Hope that comes from seeing all of this in a way that doesn't take away what's hard, or even painful, but puts it in the context of a larger story about God's commitment to us—to me, to my parents, siblings, and friends, to all of us.

I think that's what faith does. It gives us a way to keep our footing in the meantime.

And not just keep our footing, but live, and love, and try, and care. Maybe not seeing it all work out, but having hope and confidence that it will. Yeah, I think that's what I find appealing and why I can say I believe.

Then I guess there's not much more to say at this point.

What, no more theology, no more talking about God?

There's always more room for the God-talk that is theology. And I'll always look forward to doing that with you. But what I really mean is that once you're ready to get into the story, then all of our theological talk—as interesting, helpful, and even fun as it is—becomes kind of secondary. It is reflection on the more primary God-talk—that is, really talking to God through worship, prayer, and a life of service, a life lived in and according to the story we've been thinking through.

Yes. That sounds good, and just what I'm ready for.

Insights and Questions

For Further Reading

Bell, Rob and Golden, Don. *Jesus Wants to Save Christians: A Manifesto for the Church in Exile*. Grand Rapids: Zondervan, 2008.

Borg, Marcus. *The Heart of Christianity*. San Francisco: HarperOne, 2004.

Clayton, Philip. *Transforming Christian Theology for Church and Society*. Minneapolis: Fortress Press, 2010.

Forde, Gerhard. *Where God Meets Man*. Minneapolis: Augsburg Books, 1972.

Jacobson, Rolf A., ed. *Crazy Talk: A Not-So-Stuffy Dictionary of Theological Terms*. Minneapolis: Augsburg Books, 2008.

Keller, Catherine. *On the Mystery*. Minneapolis: Fortress Press, 2008.

Killen, Patricia O'Connell and de Beer, John. *The Art of Theological Reflection*. New York: The Crossroad Publishing Company, 1994.

Lewis, C.S. *Mere Christianity*. San Francisco: HarperOne, 2001.

Lose, David J. *Making Sense of Scripture*. Minneapolis: Augsburg Fortress, 2009.

Placher, William. *Narrative of a Vulnerable God: Christ, Theology, and Scripture.* Louisville: Westminster/John Knox, 1994.

Soelle, Dorothy. *Theology for Skeptics.* Minneapolis: Fortress Press, 2005.

Stone, Howard W. and Duke, James O. *How to Think Theologically.* Minneapolis: Fortress Press, 2006.

White, Michael Cooper. The *Comeback God: A Theological Primer for the Life of Faith.* Minneapolis: Fortress Press, 2009.

Wright, N. T. *Simply Christian.* San Francisco: HarperOne, 2010.